ISBN 978-1-330-84752-7
PIBN 10113281

Forgotten Books is a registered trademark of FB &c Ltd.
Copyright © 2018 FB &c Ltd.
FB &c Ltd, Dalton House, 60 Windsor Avenue, London, SW19 2RR.
Company number 08720141. Registered in England and Wales.

For support please visit www.forgottenbooks.com

1 MONTH OF
FREE
READING

at

www.ForgottenBooks.com

By purchasing this book you are eligible for one month membership to ForgottenBooks.com, giving you unlimited access to our entire collection of over 1,000,000 titles via our web site and mobile apps.

To claim your free month visit:

www.forgottenbooks.com/free113281

HISTORY

OF

NEW TESTAMENT CRITICISM

BY

F. C. CONYBEARE, M.A.

LATE FELLOW AND PRAELECTOR OF UNIV. COLL., OXFORD
FELLOW OF THE BRITISH ACADEMY; DOCTOR OF THEOLOGY
honoris causa, OF GIESSEN; OFFICIER D'ACADÉMIE

WITH ILLUSTRATIONS

G. P. PUTNAM'S SONS
NEW YORK AND LONDON
The Knickerbocker Press
1910

ERASMUS

HISTORY

OF

NEW TESTAMENT
CRITICISM

BY

F. C. CONYBEARE, M.A.

LATE FELLOW AND PRAELECTOR OF UNIV. COLL., OXFORD
FELLOW OF THE BRITISH ACADEMY; DOCTOR OF THEOLOGY
honoris causa, **OF GIESSEN; OFFICIER D'ACADÉMIE**

WITH ILLUSTRATIONS

G. P. PUTNAM'S SONS

NEW YORK AND LONDON

The Knickerbocker Press

1910

COPYRIGHT, 1910

BY

G. P. PUTNAM'S SONS

This series is published in London by
THE RATIONALIST PRESS ASSOCIATION, LIMITED

The Knickerbocker Press, New York

PUBLISHERS' NOTE

A HISTORY OF THE SCIENCES has been planned to present for the information of the general public a historic record of the great divisions of science. Each volume is the work of a writer who is accepted as an authority on his own subject-matter. The books are not to be considered as primers, but present thoroughly digested information on the relations borne by each great division of science to the changes in human ideas and to the intellectual development of mankind. The monographs explain how the principal scientific discoveries have been arrived at and the names of the workers to whom such discoveries are due.

The books will comprise each about 200 pages. Each volume will contain from 12 to 16 illustrations, including portraits of the discoverers and explanatory views and diagrams. Each volume contains also a concise but comprehensive bibliography of the subject-matter. The following volumes will be issued during the course of the autumn of 1909.

The History of Astronomy.

By GEORGE FORBES, M.A., F.R.S., M. Inst. C.E.; author of *The Transit of Venus*, etc.

**The History of Chemistry: Vol. I. circa 2000 B.C.
to 1850 A.D.   Vol. II. 1850 A.D. to date.**

By SIR EDWARD THORPE, C.B., LL.D., F.R.S.,
Director of the Government Laboratories,
London; Professor-elect and Director of
the Chemical Laboratories of the Imperial
College of Science and Technology; author
of *A Dictionary of Applied Chemistry.*

To be followed by:

The History of Geography.

By Dr. JOHN SCOTT KELTIE, F.R.G.S., F.S.S.,
F.S.A., Hon. Mem. Geographical Societies
of Paris, Berlin, Rome, Brussels, Amsterdam, Geneva. etc.; author of *Report on
Geographical Education, Applied Geography.*

The History of Geology.

By HORACE B. WOODWARD, F.R.S., F.G.S.,
Assistant-Director of Geological Survey of
England and Wales; author of *The Geology
of England and Wales*, etc.

The History of Anthropology.

By A. C. HADDON, M.A., Sc.D., F.R.S., Lecturer in Ethnology, Cambridge and London; author of *Study of Man, Magic and
Fetishism*, etc.

The History of Old Testament Criticism.

By ARCHIBALD DUFF, Professor of Hebrew
and Old Testament Theology in the United

College, Bradford; author of *Theology and Ethics of the Hebrews, Modern Old Testament Theology*, etc.

The History of New Testament Criticism.

By F. C. CONYBEARE, M.A., late Fellow and Praelector of Univ. Coll., Oxford; Fellow of the British Academy; Doctor of Theology, *honoris causa*, of Giessen; Officer d' Academie; author of *Old Armenian Texts of Revelation*, etc.

Further volumes are in plan on the following subjects:

Mathematics and Mechanics.

Molecular Physics, Heat, Life, and Electricity.

Human Physiology, Embryology, and Heredity.

Acoustics, Harmonics, and the Physiology of Hearing, together with Optics Chromatics, and Physiology of Seeing.

Psychology, Analytic, Comparative, and Experimental.

Sociology and Economics.

Ethics.

Comparative Philology.

Criticism, Historical Research, and Legends.

Comparative Mythology and the Science of Religions.

The Criticism of Ecclesiastical Institutions.

Culture, Moral and Intellectual, as Reflected in
Imaginative Literature and in the Fine Arts.

Logic.

Philosophy.

Education.

PREFACE

THE least unkind of my critics will probably find two faults with this work: firstly, that it is sketchy, and, secondly, that it says too little of the history of textual criticism and of the manuscripts and versions in which the New Testament has come down to us.

I must plead in excuse that I could do no more in so short a book, and that it is in any case not intended for specialists, but for the wider public. Within its limits there is no room to enumerate one half of the important commentaries and works of learning about the New Testament which have been produced in the last two hundred years. The briefest catalogue of these would have filled a volume four times as large. I had, therefore, to choose between a bare enumeration of names and titles, and a sketch of a movement of thought conducted by a few prominent scholars and critics. I chose the latter. Writing for English readers, I have also endeavoured to bring into prominence the work of English writers; and, in general, I have singled out for notice courageous writers who,

besides being learned, were ready to face obloquy
and unpopularity; for, unhappily, in the domain
of Biblical criticism it is difficult to please the
majority of readers without being apologetic in
tone and "goody-goody." A worker in this
field who finds himself praised by such journals
as the *Saturday Review* or the *Church Times*
may instantly suspect himself of being either
superstitious or a time-server.

So much in defence of myself from the first
charge. As to the second, I would have liked
to relate the discovery of many important
manuscripts, and to describe and appraise the
ancient versions—Latin, Syriac, Armenian,
Gothic, Georgian, Coptic, Ethiopic, and Arabic
—to the exploration of which I have devoted
many years. I would also have loved to bring
before my readers the great figures of Tyndale,
Erasmus, Beza, Voss, Grotius, Wetstein, Griesbach, Matthæi, Tischendorf, Lachmann, Scrivener, Lightfoot, and other eminent translators,
editors, and humanists. But it was useless to
explore this domain except in a separate volume
relating the history, not of New Testament
criticism in general, but of textual criticism in
particular.

F. C. C.

September, 1910.

CONTENTS

Contents

Contents

ILLUSTRATIONS

The portraits of Baur, Herder, Renan, and Luther are reproduced from prints published by the Berlin Photographic Company, London, W. The portrait of Dr. Westcott is reproduced by permission of Messrs. J. Russell & Sons; that of Dr. Burgon was supplied by Messrs. Hills & Saunders.

HISTORY OF NEW TESTAMENT CRITICISM

CHAPTER I

ANCIENT EXEGESIS

THE various writings—narrative, epistolary, and apocalyptic—which make up the New Testament had no common origin, but were composed at different times by at least a score of writers in places which, in view of the difficulties presented to travel by the ancient world, may be said to have been widely remote from each other. With the exception of the Epistles of Paul, none of them, or next to none, were composed until about fifty years after the death of Jesus; and another hundred years elapsed before they were assembled in one collection and began to take their place alongside of the Greek translation of the Hebrew Bible as authoritative scriptures.

Nor was it without a struggle that many of

them made their way into the charmed circle
of the Christian canon, or new instrument, as
Tertullian, about the year 200, called the new
sacred book; and this point is so important that
we must dwell upon it more in detail. For
the discussions in the second and early third
centuries of the age and attribution of several
of these books constitute a first chapter in the
history of New Testament criticism, and sixteen
centuries flowed away before a second was
added.

We learn, then, from Eusebius that the writings which pass under the name of John the son
of Zebedee were for several generations viewed
with suspicion, not by isolated thinkers only,
but by wide circles of believers.　These writings
comprise the fourth gospel, three epistles closely
resembling that gospel in style and thought, and,
thirdly, the Book of Revelation.　Between the
years 170 and 180 there was a party in the
Church of Asia Minor that rejected all these
writings.　The gospel of John, they argued, was
a forgery committed by a famous heretic named
Cerinthus, who denied the humanity of Jesus;
it also contradicted the other three gospels in
extending the ministry over three years, and
presented the events of his life in a new and
utterly false sequence, detailing two passovers
in the course of his ministry where the three
synoptic gospels mention only one, and ignoring

the forty days' temptation in the wilderness. About the year 172 a Bishop of Hierapolis in Asia Minor, named Claudius Apollinaris, wrote that the gospels seemed to conflict with one another, in that the synoptics give one date for the Last Supper and the fourth gospel another. Nor was it only in Asia Minor that this gospel, an early use of which can be traced only among the followers of the notable heretics Basilides and Valentinus, excited the repugnance of the orthodox; for a presbyter of the Church of Rome named Gaius, or Caius, assailed both it and the Book of Revelation, which purported to be by the same author, in a work which Hippolytus, the Bishop of Ostia, tried to answer about the year 234. We may infer that at that date there still were in Rome good Christians who accepted the views of Gaius; otherwise it would not have been necessary to refute him.

The gospel, however, succeeded in establishing itself along with the other three; and Irenæus, the Bishop of Lugdunum, or Lyon, in Gaul, soon after 174 A.D., argues that there must be four gospels, neither more nor less, because there are four corners of the world and four winds. Tatian, another teacher of the same age, also accepted it, and included it in a harmony of the four gospels which he made called the Diatessaron. This harmony was translated into Syriac, and read out loud in the churches of

Syria as late as the beginning of the fourth century.

After the age of Hippolytus no further questions were raised about the fourth gospel. Epiphanius, indeed, who died in 404, and was Bishop of Salamis in Cyprus, devotes a chapter of his work upon Heresies to the sect of *Alogi*— that is, of those who, in rejecting the fourth gospel, denied that Jesus was the *Logos* or Word of God; but by that time the question had no more than an antiquarian interest.

Not so with the Apocalypse, against which Dionysius, Patriarch, or Pope, of Alexandria in the years 247–265, wrote a treatise which more than any other work of the ancient Church approaches in tone and insight the level of modern critical research, and of which, happily, Eusebius of Cæsarea has preserved an ample fragment in his history of the Church:

> In any case [writes Dionysius], I cannot allow that the author of the Apocalypse is that Apostle, the son of Zebedee and brother of James, to whom belong the Gospel entitled *According to John* and the general Epistle. For I clearly infer, no less from the character and literary style of the two authors than from tenor of the book, that they are not one and the same.

Then he proceeds to give reasons in support of his judgment:

For the evangelist nowhere inscribes his name in his work nor announces himself either through his gospel or his epistle[1] . . . whereas the author of the Apocalypse at the very beginning thereof puts himself forward and says: The Revelation of Jesus Christ which he gave him to show to his servants speedily, and signified by his angel to his servant John, etc.

Lower down he writes thus:

And also from the thoughts and language and arrangement of words we can easily conjecture that the one writer is separate from the other. For the Gospel and the Epistle harmonise with each other and begin in the same way, the one: *In the beginning was the Word;* and the other: *That which was from the beginning.* In the one we read: *And the Word was made flesh and dwelled among us; and we beheld his glory, glory as of the only-begotten by the Father;* and the other holds the same language slightly changed: *That which we have heard, that which we have seen with our eyes, that which we beheld and our hands handled, about the Word of Life, and the life was manifested.* For this is his prelude, and such his contention, made clear in the sequel, against those who denied that the Lord came in the flesh; and therefore he adds of set purpose the words: And to what we saw we bear witness, and announce to you the eternal life which was with the

[1] Dionysius had never heard of the second and third Epistles of John.

Father and was manifested to us. What we have seen and heard we announce to you. The writer is consistent with himself, and never quits his main propositions; indeed, follows up his subject all through without changing his catchwords, some of which we will briefly recall. A careful reader, then [of the Gospel and Epistle], will find in each frequent mention of Light, Life, of flight from darkness; constant repetition of the words Truth, Grace, Joy, Flesh and Blood of the Lord, of Judgment and Remission of Sins, of God's love to usward, of the command that we love one another, of the injunction to keep all the commandments, of the world's condemnation and of the Devil's, of the Antichrist, of the Promise of the Holy Spirit, of God's Adoption of us, of Faith perpetually demanded of us. The union of Father and Son pervades both works (*i.e.*, Gospel and Epistle of John), and, if we scan their character all through, the sense is forced on us of one and the same complexion in Gospel and Epistle. But the Apocalypse stands in absolute contrast to each. It nowhere touches or approaches either of them, and, we may fairly say, has not a single syllable in common with them; any more than the Epistle—not to mention the Gospel—contains reminiscence or thought of the Apocalypse, or Apocalypse of Epistle; although Paul in his epistles hinted details of his apocalypses (*i.e.*, revelations), without writing them down in a substantive book. Moreover, we can base a conclusion on the contrast of style there is between Gospel and Epistle on the one side, and Apocalypse on the other. For the former not only use the Greek language without stumbling, but are throughout written with great elegance of diction, of reasoning and arrangement of expressions. We are far from meeting in them with barbarous words and solecisms, or any vulgarisms whatever; for their writer had both gifts, because the Lord endowed him with each, with that of knowledge and that of eloquence. I do not deny to the other his having received the gifts of knowledge and prophecy, but I cannot discern in him an exact knowledge of Greek language and tongue. He not only uses barbarous idioms, but sometimes falls into actual solecisms; which, however, I need not now detail, for my remarks are not intended to make fun of him—far be it from me—but only to give a correct idea of the dissimilitude of these writings.

Modern divines attach little weight to this well-reasoned judgment of Dionysius; perhaps because among us Greek is no longer a living language. They forget that Dionysius lived less than one hundred and fifty years later than the authors he here compares, and was therefore as well qualified to distinguish between them as we are to distinguish between Lodowick Muggleton and Bishop Burnet. We should have no difficulty in doing so, and yet they are further from us by a hundred years than these authors were from Dionysius. Whether or no the fourth gospel was a work of the Apostle John, the conclusion stands that it cannot be from the hand which penned Revelation. This conclusion Eusebius, the historian of the Church, espoused, and, following him, the entire Eastern Church; nor was the authority of Revelation rehabilitated in the Greek world before the end of the seventh century, while the outlying Churches of Syria and Armenia hardly admitted it into their canons before the thirteenth. In Rome, however, and generally in the West, where it circulated in a Latin version which disguised its peculiar idiom, it was, so far as we know, admitted into the canon from the first, and its apostolic authorship never impugned.

The early Fathers seldom display such critical ability as the above extract reveals in the case of Dionysius. Why, it may be asked, could so keen a discrimination be exercised in this particular and nowhere else? What was there to awake and whet the judgment here, when in respect of other writings it continued to slumber and sleep? The context in Eusebius's pages reveals to us the cause. The more learned and sober circles of believers had, in the last quarter of the second and the first of the third centuries, wearied and become ashamed of the antics of the Millennarists, who believed that Jesus Christ was to come again at once and establish, not in a vague and remote heaven,

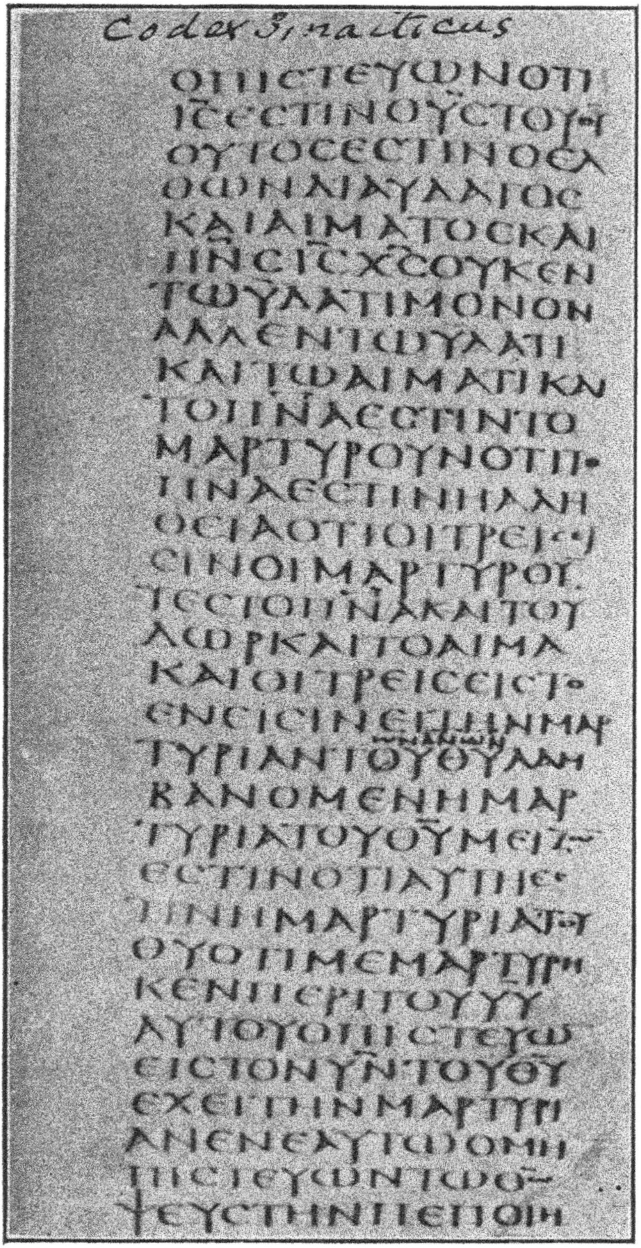

but on this earth itself, a reign of peace, plenty, and carnal well-being. ˙ These enthusiasts appealed to the Apocalypse when their dreams were challenged; and the obvious way to silence them was to prove that that book possessed no apostolic authority.   The Millennarists might have retorted, and their retort would have been true, that if one of the books was to go, then the gospel must go, on the ground that the Apostle John, whom the Epistle to the Galatians reveals as a Judaising Christian, could not possibly have written it, though he might well have penned the Apocalypse.   The age was of course too ignorant and uncritical for such an answer to suggest itself; but the entire episode serves to illustrate a cardinal principle of human nature, which is, that we are never so apt to discover the truth as when we have an outside reason for doing so, and in religion especially are seldom inclined to abandon false opinions except in response to material considerations.

Two other Christian Fathers have a place in the history of textual criticism of the New Testament—Origen and Jerome.   The former of these was not a critic in our sense of the word. He notices that there was much variety of text between one manuscript and another, but he seems seldom to have asked himself which of the two variants was the true one.   For example, in Hebrews ii., 9, he notices that in some MSS.

the text ran thus: *that by the grace of God he* (Jesus) *should taste death*, but in others thus: *that without God he should*, etc. He professes himself quite content to use either. In a few cases he corrects a place name, not from the evidence of the copies, but because of the current fashion of his age. Thus in Matthew viii., 28, the scene of the swine driven by demons into the lake was in some MSS. fixed at Gerasa, in others at Gadara. But in Origen's day pilgrims were shown the place of this miracle at Gergesa, and accordingly he was ready to correct the text on their evidence, as if it was worth anything. One other reason he adds for adopting the reading Gergesa, very characteristic of his age. It amounts to this, that the name Gergesa means in Hebrew "the sojourning-place of them that cast out"; and that divine Providence had allotted this name to the town because the inhabitants were so scared by the miracle of the swine that they exhorted Jesus to quit their confines without delay!

One other example may be advanced of Origen's want of critical acumen. In Matthew, xxvii., 17, he decided against the famous reading Jesus Barabbas as the name of the brigand who was released instead of Jesus of Nazareth, on the ground that a malefactor had no right to so holy a name as Jesus.

Origen's defence of allegory as an aid to the

interpretation no less of the New than of the Old Testament forms a curious chapter in the history of criticism.

Marcion, in the middle of the second century, had pitilessly assailed the God of the Jews, and denounced the cruelty, lust, fraud, and rapine of the Hebrew patriarchs and kings, the favourites of that God. In the middle of the third century the orthodox were still hard put to it to meet the arguments of Marcion, and, as Milton has it, "to justify the ways of God to men." Origen, learned teacher as he was, saw no way out of the difficulty other than to apply that method of allegory which Philo had applied to the Old Testament; and in his work, *On First Principles*, book iv., we have an exposition of the method. He premises, firstly, that the Old Testament is divinely inspired, because its prophecies foreshadow Christ; and, secondly, that there is not either in Old or New Testament a single syllable void of divine meaning and import. But how, he asks (in book iv. chap. 17), can we conciliate with this tenet of their entire inspiration the existence in the Bible of such tales as that of Lot and his daughters, of Abraham prostituting first one wife and then another, of a succession of at least three days and nights before the sun was created? Who, he asks, will be found idiot enough to believe that God planted trees in Paradise like any husbandman; that he set up in it visible and palpable tree-trunks, labelled the one "Tree of Life," and the other "Tree of Knowledge of Good and Evil," both bearing real fruit that might be masticated with corporeal teeth; that he went and walked about the garden; that Adam hid under a tree; that Cain fled from the face of God? The wise reader, he remarks, may well ask what the face of God is, and how any one could get away from it? Nor, he continues, is the Old Testament only full of such incidents, as no one regardful of good sense and reason can suppose to have really taken place or to be sober history. In the Gospels equally, he declares, such narratives abound; and as an example he instances the story of the Devil plumping Jesus down on the top of a lofty mountain, from which he showed him all the kingdoms of the earth and their glory. How, he asks, can it be literally true, how a historical fact, that from a single mountain-top with fleshly eyes all the realms of Persia, of Scythia, and of India could be seen adjacent and at once? The careful reader will, he says, find in the Gospels any number of cases similar to the above. In a subsequent paragraph he instances more passages which it is absurd to take in their literal sense. Such is the text Luke x., 4, in which Jesus when he sent forth the Twelve Apostles bade them "Salute no man on the way." None but silly people, he adds, believe that our Saviour delivered such a precept to the Apostles. And how, he goes on, particularly in a land where winter bristles with icicles and is bitter with frosts, could any one be asked to do with only two tunics and no shoes? And then that other command that a man who is smitten on the right cheek shall also turn the left to the smiter—how can it be true, seeing that any one who smites another with his right hand must necessarily smite his left cheek and not his right? And another of the things to be classed among the impossible is the prescription found in the Gospel, that if thy right eye offend thee it shall be plucked out. For even if we take this to apply to our bodily eyes, how is it to be considered consistent, whereas we use both eyes to see, to saddle one eye only with the guilt of the stumbling-block, and why the right eye rather. than the left?

Wherever, he argues (chap. 15), we meet with such useless, nay impossible, incidents and precepts as these, we must discard a literal interpretation and consider of what moral interpretation they are capable, with what higher and mysterious meaning they are fraught, what deeper truths they were intended symbolically and in allegory to shadow forth. The divine wisdom has of set purpose contrived these little traps and stumbling-blocks in order to cry halt to our slavish historical understanding of the text, .by inserting in its midst sundry things that are impossible and unsuitable. The Holy Spirit so waylays us in order that we may be driven by passages which taken in their *prima-facie* sense cannot be true or useful, to search for the ulterior truth, and seek in the Scriptures which we believe to be inspired by God a meaning worthy of Him.

In the sequel it occurs to Origen that some of his readers may be willing to tolerate the application of this method to the Old Testament, and yet shrink from applying it wholesale to the New. He reassures them by insisting on what Marcion had denied—namely, on the fact that the same Spirit and the same God inspired both Old and New alike, and in the same manner. Whatever, therefore, is legitimate in regard to the one is legitimate in regard to the other also. "Wherefore also in the Gospels and Epistles the Spirit has introduced not a few incidents which, by breaking in upon and checking the historical character of the narrative, with which it is impossible to reconcile them, turn back and recall the attention of the reader to an examination of their inner meaning."

Origen admits (chap. 19) that the passages in Scripture which bear a spiritual sense and no other are considerably outnumbered by those which stand good as history. Let no one, he pleads, suspect us of asserting that we think none of the Scriptural narratives to be historically true, because we suspect that some of the events related never really happened. On the contrary, we are assured that in the case of as many as possible their historical truth can be and must be upheld. Moreover, of the precepts delivered in the Gospel it cannot be doubted that very many are to ˙be literally observed, as when it says: *But I say unto you, Swear not at all.* At the same time, any one who reads carefully will be sure to feel a doubt whether this and that narrative is to be regarded as literally true or only half true, and whether this and that precept is to be literally observed or not. Wherefore with the utmost study and pains we must strive to enable every single reader with all reverence to understand that in dealing with the contents of the sacred books he handles words which are divine and not human.

It is curious in the above to note that the one precept on the literal observance of which Origen insists—namely, the prohibition of oaths —is just that which for centuries all Christian sects, with the exception of the medieval Cathars and modern Quakers, have flouted and defied. This by the way. It is more important to note how these chapters of Origen impress a would-be liberal Anglican divine of to-day.

"In reading most of Origen's difficulties," writes Dean Farrar in his *History of Interpretation*, p. 193, "we stand amazed. . . . By the slightest application of literary criticism they vanish at a touch." And just above, p. 190: "The errors of the exegesis which Origen tended to establish for more than a thousand years had their root in the assumption that the Bible is throughout homogeneous and in every particular supernaturally perfect." And again, p. 196: "Having started with the assumption that every clause of the Bible was infallible, supernatural, and divinely dictated, and having proved to his own satisfaction that it could not be intended in its literal sense, he proceeded to systematise his own false conclusions."

No doubt such criticisms are just, but did the antecedents of Dean Farrar entitle him to pass them upon Origen, who was at least as responsive to the truth as in his age any man could be expected to be? In reading these pages of the modern ecclesiastic we are reminded of the picture in the Epistle of James i., 23, of him "who is a hearer of the word and not a doer: he is like unto a man beholding his horoscope in a divining crystal (*or* mirror); for he beholdeth himself, and goeth away, and straightway forgetteth what manner of man he was."

Jerome, who was born about 346, and died 420, deserves our respect because he saw the necessity of basing the Latin Bible not upon the Septuagint or Greek translation, but upon the Hebrew original. It illustrates the manners of the age that when he was learning Hebrew, in which for his time he made himself extraordinarily proficient, the Jewish rabbis who were his teachers had to visit him by night, for fear of scandal. In this connection Jerome compares himself to Christ visited by Nicodemus. It certainly needed courage in that, as in subsequent ages, to undertake to revise a sacred text in common use, and Jerome reaped from his task much immediate unpopularity. His revision, of course, embraced the New as well as the Old Testament, but his work on the New contained nothing very new or noteworthy.

CHAPTER II

THE HARMONISTS

THE sixth article of the Church of England lays it down that "Holy Scripture containeth all things necessary to salvation," which is not the same thing as to say that everything contained in Holy Scripture is necessary to salvation. Nevertheless, this in effect has been the dominant view of the reformed churches. Underneath the allegorical method of interpreting the Bible, which I have exemplified from the works of Origen, lay the belief that every smallest portion of the text is inspired; for, apart from this belief, there was no reason not to set aside and neglect passages that in their literal and primary sense seemed unhistorical and absurd, limiting the inspiration to so much of the text as could reasonably be taken for true. The Reformation itself predisposed those churches which came under its influence to accept the idea of verbal inspiration; for, having quarrelled with the Pope, and repudiated his authority as an interpreter of the text and arbiter of difficulties arising out of it, they had no

•

oracle left to appeal to except the Bible, and they fondly imagined that they could use it as a judge uses a written code of law. As such a code must be consistent with itself, and free from internal contradictions, in order to be an effective instrument of government and administration, so must the Bible; and before long it was felt on all sides to be flat blasphemy to impute to a text which was now called outright "the Word of God" any inconsistencies or imperfections. The Bible was held by Protestants to be a homogeneous whole dictated to its several writers, who were no more than passive organs of the Holy Spirit and amanuenses of God. "Scripture," wrote Quenstedt (1617–1688), a pastor of Wittenberg, "is a fountain of infallible truth, and exempt from all error; every word of it is absolutely true, whether expressive of dogma, of morality, or of history."

Such a view left to Protestants no loophole of allegory, and their divines have for generations striven to reconcile every one statement in the Bible with every other by harmonistic shifts and expedients which, in interpreting other documents, they would disdain to use. Of these forced methods of explanation it is worth while to examine a few examples, for there is no better way of realising how great an advance has been made towards enlightenment in the present age. Our first example shall be taken from a work entitled *A Harmony of the Four Evangelists*, which was published in 1702 by William Whiston (1667–1752), a man of vast and varied attainments. A great mathematician, he succeeded Sir Isaac Newton in the Lucasian chair at Cambridge, but was deprived of it in 1710 for assailing in print the orthodox doctrine of the Trinity. In his old age he quitted the ranks of the English clergy, because he disliked the so-called Athanasian Creed, and became an Anabaptist. He was deeply read in the Christian Fathers, and was the author of many theological works. It marks the absolute sway over men's minds in that epoch of the dogma of the infallibility and verbal inspiration of the Bible that so vigorous and original a thinker as Whiston could imagine that he had reconciled by such feeble devices the manifold contradictions of the Gospels. Take, for example, the seventh of the principles or rules he formulated to guide students in harmonising them. It runs as follows:

> P. 118, vii.—The resemblance there is between several discourses and miracles of our Saviour in the several Gospels, which the order of the evangelical history places at different times, is no sufficient reason for the superseding such order, and supposing them to be the very same discourses and miracles.

He proceeds to give examples for the application of the above rule. The first of them is as follows:

> Thus it appears that our Saviour gave almost the very same instructions to the Twelve Apostles, and to the Seventy Disciples, at their several missions; the one recorded by St. Matthew, the other by St. Luke, as the likeness of the occasions did require. Now these large instructions, being in two Gospels, have been by many refer'd to the same time, by reason of their similitude.

That the reader may judge for himself how absurdly inadequate this explanation is, the two resembling discourses are here set out in opposing columns:

Luke x., 1: Now after these things the Lord appointed seventy others, and sent them two and two before his face into every city and place, whither he himself was about to come. And he said unto them, The harvest is plenteous, but the labourers are few: pray ye therefore the Lord of the harvest, that he send forth labourers into his harvest. Go your ways:

Matthew x., 1: And he called unto him his twelve disciples, and gave them authority. . . .
5: These twelve Jesus sent forth, and charged them, saying. . . .
Matthew ix., 37: Then saith he unto his disciples, The harvest, etc. . . .
(Identical as far as "into his harvest.")

Matthew x., 16: Be-

behold, I send you forth as lambs in the midst of wolves. Carry no purse, no wallet, no shoes: and salute no man on the way. And into whatsoever house ye shall enter, first say, Peace be to this house. And if a son of peace be there, your peace shall rest upon him: but if not, it shall turn to you again. . . . But into whatsoever city ye shall enter, and they receive you not, go out into the streets thereof and say, Even the dust from your city, that cleaveth to our feet, we do wipe off against you: howbeit know this, that the kingdom of God is come nigh. I say unto you, It shall be more tolerable in that day for Sodom, than for that city.

hold, I send you forth as sheep in the midst of wolves.

9, 10: Get you no gold, nor silver, nor brass in your purses; no wallet for journey, neither two coats, nor shoes nor staff: for the labourer is worthy of his food. 11: And into whatsoever city or village ye shall enter, search out who in it is worthy; and there abide till ye go forth. 12: And as ye enter the house, salute it. 13: And if the house be worthy, let your peace come upon it: but if it be not worthy, let your peace return to you. 14: And whosoever shall not receive you, nor hear your words, as ye go forth out of that house or that city, shake off the dust of your feet. 15: Verily I say unto you, It shall be more tolerable for the land of Sodom and Gomorrah in the day of judgment than

> for that city. 7: And as ye go, preach, saying, The kingdom of heaven is at hand.

Dean Alford, in his edition of the New Testament which appeared in 1863, begins his commentary on Luke x. as follows:

> Verses 1-16. Mission of the Seventy.— It is well that Luke has given us also the sending of the *Twelve*, or we should have had some of the commentators asserting that this was *the same* mission. The discourse addressed to the Seventy is in substance the same as that to the Twelve, as the similarity of their errand would lead us to suppose it would be.

But we know only what was the errand of the seventy from the instructions issued to them, and, apart from what Jesus here tells them to do, we cannot say what they were intended to do. Were there any mention of them in the rest of the New Testament, we might form some idea apart from this passage of Luke of what their mission was, but neither in the Acts is allusion to them nor in the Paulines. It was assumed long afterwards, in the fourth century, when a fanciful list of their names was concocted, that they were intended to be missionaries to the Gentiles, who were, in the current folklore of Egypt and Palestine, divided into seventy or seventy-two races; but this assumption conflicts with the statement that they were to go in front of Jesus to the several cities and places which he himself meant to visit. Alford, therefore, argues in a circle, and we can only infer that their mission was similar to that of the Twelve, because their marching orders were so similar, and not that their orders were similar because their mission was so.

In point of fact, we must take this passage of Luke in connection with other passages in which his language tallies with that of Matthew. Practically every critic, even the most orthodox, admits to-day that Matthew and Luke, in composing their Gospels, used two chief sources— one the Gospel of Mark, very nearly in the form in which we have it; and the other a document which, because Mark reveals so little knowledge of it, is called the non-Marcan document, and by German scholars *Q*—short for *Quelle* or source. By comparing those portions of Matthew and Luke which, like the two just cited, reveal, not mere similarity, but in verse after verse are identical in phrase and wording, we are able to reconstruct this lost document, which consisted almost wholly of teachings and sayings of Jesus, with very few narratives of incidents. The Lucan text before us is characterised by exactly the same degree of approximation to Matthew's text which we find in other passages; for example, in those descriptive of the temptation of Jesus—namely, Luke iv., 1–13 = Matthew iv., 1–11. There also, however, Alford, incurably purblind, asserts (note on Luke iv., 1) that "The accounts of Matthew and Luke (Mark's is principally a compendium) are distinct." He refers us in proof of this assertion to his notes on Matthew and Mark, although in those notes he has made no attempt to substantiate it.

In the present day, then, it is flogging a dead horse to controvert Dean Alford or William Whiston on such a point as this. The standpoint of orthodox criticism in the twentieth century is well given in a useful little book entitled *The Study of the Gospels*, by J. Armitage Robinson, D.D., Dean of Westminster (London, 1902). On p. 111 of this book there is a table of certain passages which Luke and Matthew derived in common from the non-Marcan document, and one of its items is the following:

Luke x., 1–12. Mission of seventy disciples = Matt. ix., 37 *ff.*, x. 1 *ff.*

And, again, p. 112:

Thus in ix., 35–x., 42 he [Matthew] has combined the charge to the twelve (Mark vi., 7 *ff.*) with the charge to the seventy, which St. Luke gives separately.

But there is a problem here over which Dr. Robinson passes in silence, though it must surely have suggested itself to his unusually

keen intelligence. It may be stated thus:
Why does Luke make two missions and two
charges, one of the Twelve Apostles, copied
directly from Mark, and the other of Seventy
Disciples, copied directly from the non-Marcan
document; whereas Matthew makes only one
mission—that of the Twelve—and includes in
the charge or body of instructions given to
them the instructions which Luke reserves for
the Seventy alone?

The question arises: Did the non-Marcan
source refer these instructions—which Luke
keeps distinct—to the Twelve, or to the Seventy,
or to no particular mission at all? Here are
three alternatives.

In favour of the second hypothesis is the fact
that later on in the same chapter—verses 17-20
—Luke narrates the return of the Seventy to
Jesus in a section which runs thus:

> And the seventy returned with joy, say-
> ing, Lord, even the devils are subject unto
> us in thy name. And he said unto them, I
> beheld Satan fallen as lightning from heaven.
> Behold, I have given you authority to tread
> upon serpents and scorpions, and over all the
> power of the enemy; and nothing shall in any
> wise hurt you, etc.

Against this second hypothesis it may be
contended that—

Firstly, if the non-Marcan source had expressly referred these instructions to the corps of Seventy Disciples, then Matthew could not have conflated them with the instructions to the Twelve which he takes from Mark vi., 7–13.

Secondly, the non-Marcan document which Luke copied in his tenth chapter was itself at the bottom identical with the text of Mark vi., 7–13, for not only are the ideas conveyed in the two the same, but the language so similar that we must infer a literary connection between them.

Thirdly, in Luke's narrative of the return of the Seventy several ideas and phrases seem to be borrowed from a source used by the author (probably Aristion, the Elder) of the last twelve verses of Mark, where they are put into the mouth of the risen Christ.

There is really but a single explanation of all these facts, and it is this: that there were two closely parallel and ultimately identical accounts of a sending forth of apostles by Jesus, one of which Mark has preserved, while the other stood in the non-Marcan document. This latter one contained precepts only, and did not specify to whom or when they were delivered. Matthew saw that they referred to one and the same event, and therefore blended them in one narrative. Luke, on the other hand, obedient to his habit of keeping separate what was in Mark from what was in the non-Marcan source, even when these two sources repeated each other verbally, assumed that the non-Marcan narrative must refer to some other mission than that of the Twelve, the account of which he had already reproduced verbally from Mark. He conjectured that as there had been a mission of twelve sent only to the twelve tribes of Israel, so there must have been a mission of seventy disciples corresponding to the seventy elders who had translated 200 years earlier the Hebrew Scriptures into Greek, and so been the means of diffusing among the Gentiles a knowledge of the old Covenant. But in that case the mission of the Seventy is pure conjecture of Luke's. With this it well agrees that outside this chapter of Luke they are nowhere else mentioned in the New Testament, and that Eusebius, the historian of the Church, searched all through the many Christian writers who preceded him in the first and second centuries—writers known to him, but lost for us—in order to find a list of these seventy disciples, but found it not. It is incredible, if they ever existed, that in all this literature there should have been no independent mention of them.

In the preceding pages I have somewhat anticipated the historical development of criticism; but it was right to do so, for it is not easy to understand its earlier stages without contrasting the later ones. The harmony of William Whiston supplies many more instances of blind adherence to the dogma that in the New Testament, as being the Word of God, there cannot be, because there must not be, any contradictions or inconsistencies of statement. It is not well, however, to dwell too long on a single writer, and I will next select an example from the *Dissertations* (Oxford, 1836) of that most learned of men, Edward Greswell, Fellow of Corpus Christi College. In these we find harmonies so forced that even Dean Alford found them excessive. Take the following as an example.

In Matthew viii., 19–22, and Luke ix., 57–60, the same pair of incidents is found in parallel texts:

Matt. viii., 19: And there came a Scribe, and said unto him, Master, I will follow thee w h i t h e r s o e v e r thou goest.

20: And Jesus saith unto him, The foxes have holes, and the birds of heaven nests; but the Son of Man hath not where to lay his head.

21: And another of the disciples said unto him, Lord, suffer me

Luke ix. 57: And as they went in the way, a certain man said unto him, I will follow thee whithersoever thou goest.

58: And Jesus said, etc. (as in Matt.).

59: And he said unto another, Follow me. But he said,

first to go and bury my father.

22: But Jesus saith unto him, Follow me; and leave the dead to bury their own dead.

Lord, suffer me first to go and bury my father.

60: But he said unto him, Leave the dead to bury their own dead; but go thou and publish abroad the kingdom of God.

Now, in Matthew the above incidents follow the descent of Jesus from the mount on which he had delivered his long sermon, separated therefrom by a series of three healings, of a leper, of a centurion's servant, and of Peter's wife's mother, and by Jesus' escape from the multitude across the lake. They therefore occurred, according to Matthew, early in the ministry of Jesus, and in Galilee, to the very north of Palestine. Luke, on the contrary, sets them late in Jesus' career, when he was on his way southward to Jerusalem, just before the crucifixion. Accordingly Greswell sets Matt. viii., 18–34 in § xx. of the third part of his harmony on November 1, A.D. 28, and Luke ix.. 57–60 in § xxv. of the fourth part, January 23, A.D. 30.

This acrobatic feat provokes even from Dean Alford the following note on Matt. viii., 19:

> Both the following incidents are placed by St. Luke long after, during our Lord's last journey to Jerusalem. For it is quite impossible (with Greswell, *Diss.*, ii., p. 155),

in any common fairness of interpretation,
to imagine that two such incidents should
have twice happened, and both times have
been related together. It is one of those
cases where the attempts of the Harmonists
do violence to every principle of sound historical criticism. Every such difficulty, instead of being a thing to be wiped out and
buried at all hazards (I am sorry to see, *e.g.*,
that Dr. Wordsworth takes no notice, either
here or in St. Luke, of the recurrence of the
two narratives), is a valuable index and
guide to the humble searcher after truth,
and is used by him as such.

And again in his prolegomena, § 4, Alford
writes of the same two passages and of other
similar parallelisms thus:

> Now the way of dealing with such dis-
> crepancies has been twofold, as remarked
> above. The *enemies of the faith* have of
> course *recognised* them, and pushed them to
> the utmost; often attempting to create them
> where they do not exist, and where they do,
> using them to overthrow the narrative in
> which they occur. While this has been
> *their* course, equally unworthy of the Evan-
> gelists and their subject has been that of
> those who are usually thought the *orthodox
> Harmonists*. They have usually taken upon
> them to state that such variously placed
> narratives *do not refer to the same incidents*,
> and so to save (as they imagine) the credit of
> the Evangelists, at the expense of common
> fairness and candour.

And below he writes:

> We need not be afraid to recognise real discrepancies, in the spirit of fairness and truth. *Christianity never was, and never can be, the gainer by any concealment, warping, or avoidance of the plain truth, wherever it is to be found.*

In the first of the above passages cited from Dean Alford, discrepancies in the Gospels are described as difficulties. But they were not such apart from the prejudice that the Bible was an infallible, uniform, and self-consistent whole. Discard this idle hypothesis, which no one ever resorted to in reading Thucydides or Herodotus, or Julius Cæsar, or the Vedas, or Homer, or any other book except the Bible, and these "difficulties" vanish. In a later section of his prolegomena, § vi., 22, Alford lays down a proposition more pregnant of meaning than he realised:

> We must take our views of inspiration not, as is too often done, from *à priori* considerations, but ENTIRELY FROM THE EVIDENCE FURNISHED BY THE SCRIPTURES THEMSELVES.

This can mean only that, since the Gospels, no less than other books of the Bible, teem with discrepancies, therefore their *plenary inspiration* (which the Dean claimed *to hold to the utmost,*

while rejecting *verbal inspiration*) is consistent
with such discrepancies; nor merely with discrepancies, but with untruths and inaccuracies
as well.   For where there are two rival and inconsistent accounts of the same fact and event
one must be true and the other false.   I do not
see how Dean Alford could, on the above
premisses, quarrel with one who should maintain that the Chronicle of Froissart or the *Acta
Sanctorum* was quite as much inspired as the
Bible. He denounces the doctrine of verbal
inspiration; that is to say, the teaching "that
every word and phrase of the Scriptures is
absolutely and separately true, and, whether
narrative or discourse, took place, or was said,
in every most exact particular as set down."
He claims to exercise "the freedom of the
Spirit" rather than submit to "the bondage of
the letter," and he justly remarks that the
advocates of verbal inspiration "must not be
allowed, with convenient inconsistency, to take
refuge in a common-sense view of the matter
wherever their theory fails them, and still to
uphold it in the main."

And yet, when we examine his commentary,
we find him almost everywhere timorous and
unscientific.   For example, the most orthodox of
modern critics frankly admits that two miracles
in Mark—that of the feeding of the four, and
that of the five, thousand—are a textual doublet;

I mean that there was one original story of the kind, which, in the hands of separate story-tellers or scribes, was varied in certain details, notably as to the place and period at which the miracle was wrought, and as to the number of people who were fed. The compiler of our second Gospel found both stories current—no doubt in two different manuscripts—and, instead of blending them into one narrative, kept them separate, under the impression that they related different incidents, and so copied them out one upon and after the other. The literary connection between these two stories *saute aux yeux*, as the French say—*leaps to the eyes.* Entire phrases of the one agree with entire phrases of the other, and the actions detailed in the one agree with and follow in the same sequence with those detailed in the other. Long before Alford's time open-eyed critics had realised that the two stories were variations of a common theme; and yet Alford, in exemplification of his canon (Chap. I., § iv., p. 5) that *Similar incidents must not be too hastily assumed to be the same*, writes as follows:

If one Evangelist had given us the feeding of the *five* thousand, and another that of the *four*, we should have been strongly tempted to pronounce the incidents the same, and to find a discrepancy in the accounts; but our conclusion would have been false, for we have now *both events* narrated by each of two Evangelists (Matthew and Mark), and formally alluded to by our Lord Himself in connexion (Matt. xvi., 9, 10; Mark viii., 19, 20).

He also, as another example of his canon's applicability, instances the stories of the anointings of the Lord at feasts, first by a woman who was a sinner, in Luke vii., 36, *ff.*, and again by Mary the sister of Lazarus, in Matt. xxvi., 6, *ff.*, and Mark xiv., 3, *ff.*, and John xi., 2, and xii., 3, *ff.* These stories are so like one another that, as Whiston observes, "the great Grotius (died 1645) himself was imposed upon, and induc'd to believe them the very same. Such fatal mistakes," he adds, "are men liable to when they indulge themselves in the liberty of changing the settled order of the Evangelists on every occasion."

The fatal mistake, of course, lay with Whiston, and with Alford, who took up the same position as he. Whiston unconsciously pays a great tribute to the shrewdness and acumen of Grotius.

Latter-day divines are somewhat contemptuous of the attitude of their predecessors fifty years ago. Thus Dr. Sanday writes in his Bampton Lectures of 1893 as follows (p. 392):

The traditional theory needs little description. Fifty years ago it may be said to have been the common belief of Christian men—at least in this country. It may have been held somewhat vaguely and indefinitely, and those who held it might, if pressed on the subject, have made concessions which would have involved them in perplexities. But, speaking broadly, the current view may be said to have been that the Bible as a whole and in all its parts was the Word of God, and as such that it was endowed with all the perfections of that Word. Not only did it disclose truths about the Divine nature and operation which were otherwise unattainable; but all parts of it were equally authoritative, and in history, as well as in doctrine, it was exempt from error. . . . This was the view commonly held fifty years ago. And when it comes to be examined, it is found to be substantially not very different from that which was held two centuries after the birth of Christ.

To this idea of verbal inspiration Dr. Sanday opposes what he calls an inductive or critical view of inspiration, in accordance with which the believer will, where the two conflict, accept "the more scientific statement." On this view the Bible is not as such inspired, and the inspiration of it is fitful, more active in one portion of it than in another. Where the two views most diverge is in the matter of the historical books. These do not always narrate plain matter of fact, as they were supposed to do formerly; nor are they "exempted from possibilities of error." Where they conflict with scientific statements they must be regarded "rather as conveying a religious lesson than as histories."

I do not grudge this writer the task of extracting religious lessons out of certain portions of the Old Testament, but it is more important to consider the implications of this modern Anglican doctrine of inspiration. Is it open to every one and any one to pick and choose and decide what in the Scriptures is true and what not, what inspired and what uninspired? Who is to be trusted with this new task of detecting an inner canon inside of the old canon of Scripture?

There is a school of thinkers inside the Church who desire to assume this task, and who never weary of insisting on the authority of the priesthood in this matter. That somewhat mordant, but not very enlightened, critic, Sir Robert Anderson, in a work entitled *The Bible and Modern Criticism* (London, 1903), not unjustly observes (p. 172) that "the Lux Mundi school has fallen back on the Church as the source of authority . . . because the Bible, so far from being infallible, is marred by error, and therefore affords no sure basis of faith." And this is undoubtedly the point of view of High Church clergymen. It remains to be seen whether in the minds of Englishmen the authority of the Church will survive that of the Bible.

CHAPTER III

THE DEISTS

THE Unitarian movement, which flourished in Poland during the sixteenth century, and penetrated to England in the seventeenth, contributed but little to the criticism of the New Testament. It is true that Lelius Socinus (1525-1562) and Faustus Socinus (1539-1604), his nephew, both of Siena, after whom the Unitarians were called Socinians, denied many tenets held to be fundamental in the great churches of east and west, such as that of the trinity and that of baptism with water; but, no more than the medieval Cathars who in both these respects anticipated them, did they dream of calling in aid the resources of textual criticism. They merely accepted the New Testament text as they found it in Erasmus's Greek edition, or even in the Latin vulgate, and accepted it as fully and verbally inspired. No more than their Calvinist and Jesuit persecutors, had they any idea of a development of church doctrine such as could have led incidentally to interpolations and alterations of the texts.

They questioned neither the traditional attributions of these texts nor their historical veracity. Nor did it ever occur even to John Locke to doubt the plenary inspiration of scripture, although his philosophy, with its rejection of authority and appeal to experience and common sense, operated strongly for the creation of that rationalistic school of thinkers who came to be known as Deists. The writers of this school, who flourished at the end of the seventeenth and during the eighteenth century, dealt with many subjects; but they all of them stood for a revolt against authority in religion. Thus Tindal, in his preface to his work, *Christianity as Old as the Creation; or, the Gospel a Republication of the Religion of Nature*, declares in his preface that:

> He builds nothing on a thing so uncertain as *tradition*, which differs in most countries; and of which, in all countries, the bulk of mankind are incapable of judging.

The scope of his work is well indicated in the headings of his chapters, one and all. Take for example this:

> Chap. I.: That God, at all times, has given mankind sufficient means of knowing whatever He requires of them, and what those means are.

And in this chapter we read:

Too great a stress can't be laid on *natural* religion; which, as I take it, differs not from *revealed*, but in the manner of its being communicated: the one being the internal, as the other the external revelation of the same unchangeable will of a Being, who is alike at all times infinitely wise and good.

This author never wearies of contrasting the simplicity of natural religion, the self-evidencing clearness of the laws of goodness, mercy, and duty impressed on all human hearts, with the complexity and uncertainty of a revelation which rests or is contained in Scriptures; and he knows how to enrol leading Anglican authorities on his side in urging his point. Thus (p. 214 of the third edition, London, 1732) he adduces a passage from the *Polemical Works* of Jeremy Taylor, which begins thus:

Since there are so many copies with infinite varieties of reading; since a various interpunction, a parenthesis, a letter, an accent, may much alter the sense; since some places have divers literal senses, many have spiritual, mystical, and allegorical meanings; since there are so many tropes, metonymies, ironies, hyperboles, proprieties and improprieties of language, whose understanding depends on such circumstances, that it is almost impossible to know the proper interpretation, now that the knowledge of such circumstances, and particular stories, is irrecoverably lost; since there are some

mysteries which, at the best advantage of
expression, are not easy to be apprehended;
and whose explication, by reason of our
imperfections, must needs be dark, sometimes unintelligible; and, lastly, since those
ordinary means of expounding Scripture, as
searching the originals, conference of places,
parity of reason, analogy of faith, are all
dubious, uncertain, and very fallible; he
that is wisest, and by consequence the like-
liest to expound truest, in all probability of
reason, will be very far from confidence.

The alternatives are thus presented of becoming "priests' worshippers," with "a divine
faith in their dictates," or of resigning oneself to
Bishop Taylor's attitude of suspense and doubt.
For as that writer concludes: "So many de-
grees of improbability and incertainty, all de-
press our certainty of finding out truth in such
mysteries." These, as. he elsewhere says
(*Polem. Works*, p. 521): "Have made it impossible for a man in so great a variety of matter
not to be deceived." The first alternative involves, as Chillingworth said in his *Religion of
Protestants*, a "deifying" by some Pope or other
of "his own interpretations and tyrannous in
forcing them upon others"; and a Pope is "the
common incendiary of Christendom," who
"tears in pieces, not the coat, but the bowels
and members of Christ: *ridente Turca, nec dolente
Iudaeo.*"

From the above extracts we can judge of
Tindal's position. He did not directly attack
orthodoxy; indeed, had he done so he could
hardly have retained his fellowship at All Souls'
College. But the direct implication of his work
throughout was this, that Christianity is not
only superfluous, but too obscure to be set on a
level with natural religion. His book is still
worth reading, and very superior to the feeble
counterblasts penned by several contemporary
divines, one of whom was my own direct
ancestor, John Conybeare, Bishop of Bristol.
Space forbids me to dwell as long as I would like
to on the work. I will only draw attention to
his acute discussion in his sixth chapter of
the intellectual preconditions of any revelation
whatever. Men, he there argues, must have
been gifted not only with an idea of a perfect
and Supreme Being, but with a certainty of his
existence, and an idea of his perfections, before
they can even approach the question, *Whether
he has made any external Revelation.* All discussion of such a question is bound to be idle
"except we could know whether this Being
is bound by his external word; and had not,
either at the time of giving it, a secret will inconsistent with his revealed will; or has not since
changed his will." The modern High Church-
man imagines that he has strengthened the
position of orthodoxy by a doctrine of pro-

gressive revelation. In other words, Jehovah, when he delivered the Law to Moses, communicated neither his true will nor the whole truth to mankind; he only did so when he sent Jesus into Judæa and founded the Christian Church and its sacraments. We may well ask with Tindal how we can be sure that the Church and its sacraments exhaust the truth. May there not still remain a *Secret Will* in reserve waiting to be revealed, as little consistent with current orthodoxy and its dogmas and rites as these are with the old Jewish religion of animal sacrifices? Of Tindal's work only the first volume was published in 1730, when he was already an old man. He died in 1733, leaving a second ready for the press. It never saw the light, for Dr. Gibson, Bishop of London, with whom Tindal had more than once crossed swords, got hold of the manuscript after the author's death, and, rightly judging that it was easier to suppress than answer such a work, had it destroyed. The late Bishop Stubbs, with unconscious humour, confesses in one of his letters to a similar action. He met John Richard Green for the first time in a railway train, and, noticing that he was reading Renan's *Life of Jesus*, engaged him in a discussion of other topics. Before the conversation ended the Bishop had transferred the obnoxious volume to his own hand-bag whence, when he reached his home, he transferred it into his waste-paper basket. So history repeats itself at long intervals. Amid the revolutions of theology little remains the same except the episcopal temper.

I have dwelt first on Matthew Tindal because his work illustrates so well the general tone of Deists. I must now turn to two of his contemporaries who are memorable for their criticisms of the New Testament.

The author of the first Gospel incessantly appends to his narratives of Jesus the tag: *Now all this is come to pass that it might be fulfilled which was spoken by the prophet.* So in Luke xxiv., 25, it is related how the risen Jesus, on the road to Emmaus, by way of convincing two of his disciples of the reality of his resurrection, said unto them, *O foolish men and slow of heart to believe in accordance with all the prophets have spoken! . . . And beginning from Moses and from all the prophets, he interpreted to them throughout the Scriptures the things concerning himself.*

And similarly in the fourth Gospel (xix., 28), Jesus, *that the Scripture might be accomplished,* said: *I thirst, . . . And when he had received the vinegar, he said, This Scripture also is fulfilled; and he bowed his head, and gave up his spirit.*[1]

[1] Here the English version, following all the MSS., renders: "He said, It is finished" (*or* fulfilled). But the

I cite these passages to illustrate the character of that form of embellishment of the narratives of Jesus to which the name of prophetic *gnosis* has been given, and which was the chief—perhaps the only—weapon of his followers against the Jews who scornfully denied him to be the Messiah.   After doing service against the Jews, the same argument was used to compel the Gentiles also to accept the new religion; and Christian literature, until the other day, largely consisted of the argument from prophecy, as it was termed.   With rabbinical ingenuity, thousands of passages were torn from the living context which gave them sense and meaning, and distorted, twisted, mutilated, misinterpreted, in order to fit them in as predictions of Jesus the Messiah.   No one thought much of what they signified in their surroundings, or, indeed, of whether they had there any rational signification at all.

Now early in the seventeenth century a few of the more intelligent students of the Bible began to express doubts about the matter. Various passages taken immemorially for prophecies of Christ seemed on closer inspection to

words survive as I have given them in Eusebius's citations of the passage and in the old Georgian version, which probably reflects the second-century Syriac version.   Their extreme frigidity would explain their omission from all the Greek MSS.

yield a better and more coherent sense if interpreted by reference to the particular portions of the Old Testament to which they belonged. Such of them as were really anticipations of a future were seen to have received their fulfilment in the close sequel of the Old Testament history; others were not anticipations at all, but statements of past events made by ancient writers. It was pointed out by scholars, who now began to familiarise themselves with that tongue, that in Hebrew the grammatical forms expressive of past and future action are almost identical, and easily mistaken for one another. Worse still, many passages of the Septuagint or old Greek translation of the Old Testament were found on examination of the Hebrew text to be mistranslations. The Hebrew original, rightly interpreted, had quite another meaning than that which the evangelists, in their ignorance of Hebrew, had blindly accepted.

William Whiston, whose harmonistic canons we have already discussed (p. 21 *ff*.), was impressed by these doubts, and set himself to resolve them. He could not, in a modern and critical manner, admit that the passages of the Old Testament adduced by the first and other evangelists as prophecies were not such, but adopted the topsy-turvy hypothesis that where the old Hebrew text did not warrant the Christian abuse of it, it had been changed and cor-

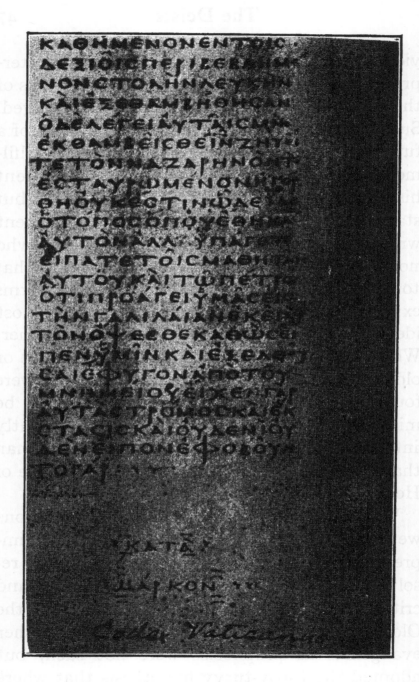

ΚΑΘΗΜΕΝΟΝΕΝΤΟΙϹ·
ΔΕΞΙΟΙϹΠΕΡΙΒΕΒλΗ
ΝΟΝϹΤΟλΗΝλΕΥΚΗΝ
ΚΑΙΕΞΕΘΑΜΒΗΘΗϹΑΝ
ΟΔΕλΕΓΕΙΑΥΤΑΙϹΜΗ
ΕΚΘΑΜΒΕΙϹΘΕΙΝΖΗΤΕΙ
ΤΕΤΟΝΝΑΖΑΡΗΝΟΝΤΟΝ
ΕϹΤΑΥΡΩΜΕΝΟΝΗΓΕΡ
ΘΗΟΥΚΕϹΤΙΝΩΔΕΙ
ΟΤΟΠΟϹΟΠΟΥΕΘΗΚΑΝ
ΑΥΤΟΝΑλλΑΥΠΑΓΕΤΕ
ΕΙΠΑΤΕΤΟΙϹΜΑΘΗΤΑΙϹ
ΑΥΤΟΥΚΑΙΤΩΠΕΤΡ
ΟΤΙΠΡΟΑΓΕΙΥΜΑϹΕΙϹ
ΤΗΝΓΑλΙλΑΙΑΝΕΚΕΙ
ΤΟΝΟΨΕϹΘΕΚΑΘΩϹ
ΠΕΝΥΜΙΝΚΑΙΕΞΕλ
ΕΙϹΕΦΥΓΟΝΑΠΟΤΟΥ
ΜΝΗΜΕΙΟΥΕΙΧΕΝΓΑ
ΑΥΤΑϹΤΡΟΜΟϹΚΑΙΕΚ
ϹΤΑϹΙϹΚΑΙΟΥΔΕΝΙΟΥ
ΔΕΝΕΙΠΟΝΕΦΟΒΟΥ
ΤΟΓΑ

ΚΑΤΑ

ΜΑΡΚΟΝ

Codex Vaticanus

MARK XVI., 5–8

rupted by Jewish enemies of Christ. In the age of the Apostles, he argued, or rather assumed, the Hebrew text had agreed with the Greek, so that they could argue from the latter taken in its literal sense. He admitted that the texts in their modern form are irreconcilable; and, having learned Hebrew, he boldly set himself to re-write the original, so as to make it tally with Christian requirements. But here a scholar as learned as himself, but less encumbered with the pedantry of orthodoxy, crossed his path. This was Anthony Collins (1676–1729), a scholar of Eton and of King's College, Cambridge. Already, in 1707, he had published a work in which he pleaded for "the use of Reason in propositions the evidence whereof depends on human testimony." In 1713 he issued *A Discourse on Freethinking*, in which he showed that in every age men have been virtuous in proportion as they were enlightened and free to think for themselves. Without such freedom of thought Christianity, he said, could never have won its early victories. In these two works he hardly went beyond what his master and intimate friend John Locke might have written; and the latter, in a letter addressed to him ten years earlier, had written thus:

> Believe it, my good friend, to love truth for truth's sake is the principal part of

human perfection in this world, and the source of all other virtues: and if I mistake not, you have as much of it as ever I met with in anybody.

The above-mentioned works, and also an earlier work in 1709 entitled *Priestcraft in Perfection*, raised up against Collins a plentiful crop of enemies; he had already been obliged, in 1711, to retire for a time to Holland to escape the storm. There he gained the friendship of Le Clerc (1657–1736), who as early as 1685 had openly attacked the belief in the inspiration of the Bible, as it was then and long afterwards formulated. But it was in 1724 that Collins published the work which most deeply offended. This was his *Discourse on the Grounds and Reasons of the Christian Religion*, and was called forth by the work of Whiston. The following passage sums up the results at which he arrives:

> In fine, the prophecies cited from the Old Testament by the authors of the New do so plainly relate, in their obvious and primary sense, to other matters than those which they are produced to prove, that to pretend they prove, in that sense, what they are produced to prove is (as Simon, *Bibl. Crit.*, vol. iv., p. 513, and *Histoire Crit. du Nouv. Test.*, chaps. 21 and 22, declares) *to give up the cause* of Christianity to *Jews* and other *enemies* thereof; who can so easily show, in so many undoubted instances, the

Old Testament and New Testament to have no manner of connection in that respect, but to be in an *irreconcilable state* (as Whiston said in his *Essay*, etc., p. 282).

The remedy proposed by Collins is that of allegorising the so-called prophecies, and of taking them in a secondary sense different from their obvious and literal one. In no other way, he urged, can they be adapted to the belief in the spiritual Messiah who is yet to appear; for the prophecies must have been fulfilled, or the Christian faith which they evidenced is false. Since they were demonstrably never fulfilled in their literal sense, Collins argues that the pointing of the Hebrew text must be altered, the order of words and letters transposed, words cut in half, taken away or added—any procrustean methods, in short, employed, in order to force the text into some sort of conformity with the events.

The good faith of Collins in propounding such a remedy was questioned by the many divines who undertook to answer him, and also by modern historians of the Deistic movement, like Leslie Stephen. He was accused of covertly ridiculing and destroying the Christian religion, while professing to justify and uphold it. This is a point to which I shall presently advert. For the moment let us select an example which illustrates the great sagacity and acumen he displayed in his attack on the argument from prophecy. It shall be his discussion of the text Isaiah vii., 14, invoked in Matt. i., 23: *Behold,* הנה *the virgin shall be with child, and shall bring forth* הרה *a son, etc.*

These words [wrote Collins], as they stand in Isaiah, from whom they are supposed to be taken, do, in their obvious and literal sense, relate to a *young woman* in the days of Ahaz, King of Judah.

He then shows from the context of Isaiah, chap. viii., how Ahaz

took two witnesses, and in their presence *went unto* the said virgin, or young woman, called the *Prophetess* (verse 3), who in due time conceived and bare a son, who was named Immanuel; after whose birth, the projects of Rezin and Pekah (Is. viii., 8–10) were soon confounded, according to the *Prophecy* and *Sign* given by the prophet.

The sign (Isaiah vii., 14) was

given by the prophet to convince Ahaz that he (the prophet) brought a message from the Lord to him to assure him that the two kings should not succeed against him. How could a virgin's conception and bearing a son seven hundred years afterwards be a *sign* to Ahaz that the prophet came to him with the said message from the Lord?

And how useless was it to Ahaz, as well as absurd in itself, for the prophet to say: *Before the child*, born seven hundred years hence, shall distinguish between *good* and *evil, the land shall be 'forsaken of both her kings?*—which should seem a banter, instead of a sign. But a prophecy of the certain birth of a male child to be born within a year or two seems a proper *sign.* . . .

Similarly he points out that the words of Hosea cited in Matt. ii., 15, were no prediction, but a statement of a past fact—viz., that Jehovah had brought Israel his son out of Egypt.

Collins also undertook to show that the Book of Daniel, on which his antagonist Whiston relied, was a forgery of the age of Antiochus Epiphanes. This brilliant conjecture, which modern inquiry has substantiated, of itself suffices to place him in the foremost rank of critics. Bentley, the King's librarian, indulged in gibes, as cheap as they were coarse, at Collins's mistakes in the domain of scholarship; but here was a discovery which, had Bentley known it, far outshone in importance, while it rivalled in critical insight, his own exposure in 1699 of the *Epistles of Phalaris*, the genuineness of which was at the time an article of faith in Oxford colleges.

The other writer of this age who must be set alongside of Collins as a critic of the New Testament was Thomas Woolston (1699–1731). The general position of this writer was, that the miracles related of Jesus are so unworthy of a spiritual Messiah that they must one and all, including the resurrection, be set down as never having happened at all, and be explained allegorically as types or figures of the real, which is the spiritual, alone. I reproduce in his own words, from his *Discourse on the Miracles*, sixth edition, London, 1729, p. 7, his programme:

I will show that the miracles of healing all manner of bodily diseases, which Jesus was justly famed for, are none of the proper miracles of the Messiah, nor are they so much as a good proof of Jesus' divine authority to found and introduce a religion into the world.

And to do this let us consider, first, in general, what was the opinion of the Fathers about the Evangelists, in which the life of Christ is recorded. Eucherius says that the scriptures of the New as well as Old Testament are to be interpreted in an allegorical sense. And this his opinion is no other than the common one of the first ages of the Church . . . consequently the literal story of Christ's miracles proves nothing. But let's hear particularly their opinion of the actions and miracles of our Saviour. Origen says that *whatsoever Jesus did in the flesh was but typical and symbolical of what he would do in the spirit;* and to our purpose, that *the several bodily diseases which he healed were no other than figures of the spiritual infirmities of the soul, that are to be cured by him.*

The following are some of the results at which he arrives by applying the above canon:

Jesus' feedings of five and four thousand in the wilderness "are most romantick tales."

The miracle of Mark ii., 1–12 = Luke v., 17–26 is "such a rodomontado that, were men to stretch for a wager, against reason and truth, none could outdo it."

He also banters the spittle miracle (in John ix.)

of the blind man, for whom eye-salve was made of clay and spittle; which eye-salve, whether it was Balsamick or not, does equally affect the credit of the miracle. If it was naturally medicinal, there's an end of the miracle; and if it was not medicinal, it was foolishly and impertinently apply'd, and can be no otherwise accounted for than by considering it, with the Fathers, as a figurative act in Jesus (p. 55).

Of another famous tale he writes:

Jesus' cursing the fig-tree, for its not bearing fruit out of season, upon the bare mention of it, appears to be a foolish, absurd, and ridiculous act, if not figurative. . . . It is so like the malignant practices of witches, who, as stories go, upon envy, grudge, or distaste, smite their neighbours' cattle with languishing distempers, till they die.

And thus of the Magi:

Of the Wise Men out of the East, with their (literally) senseless and ridiculous presents of frankincense and myrrh, to a new-born babe. If with their gold, which could be but little, they had brought their *dozens* of sugar, soap, and candles, which would have been of use to the child and his poor mother in the straw, they had acted like wise as well as good men (p. 56).

From the *Fourth Discourse on the Miracles*, London, 1729, p. 36, on the miracle of Cana:

Jesus, after their more than sufficient drinking for their satisfaction of nature, had never turned water into wine, nor would his mother have requested him to do it, if, I say, they had not a mind, and took pleasure in it too, to see the company quite *stitch'd up*. . . .
The Fathers of your Church, being sensible of the absurdity, abruptness, impertinence, pertness, and senselessness of the passage before us according to the letter, had recourse to a mystical and allegorical interpretation, as the only way to make it consistent with the wisdom, sobriety, and duty of the Holy Jesus (p. 35).

In his sixth discourse on the miracles Woolston assails the narratives of the Resurrection. He evidently felt that he was running some risk of prosecution and imprisonment by his freedom of speech, so he puts the chief of his argument into the mouth of an imaginary Jewish rabbi. The latter begins by lamenting the loss of the writings which, according to Justin Martyr (*c.* 130–140), his own ancestors unquestionably dispersed against Jesus. These, if we had them, would, he avers, yield us a clear insight into the cheat and imposture of the Christian religion.

He then proceeds to argue that the priests who sealed the sepulchre waited for Jesus to rise again after three days—*i.e.*, on Monday—but that the disciples stole a march on them by removing the body a day earlier, and then pretended the sense of the prophecy to be that he should rise on the third day. The disciples were

> afraid to trust Jesus' body, its full time, in the grave, because of the greater difficulty to carry it off afterwards, and pretend a resurrection upon it. . . .
>
> Jesus' body was gone betimes in the morning, before our *chief priests* could be out of their beds; and a bare-faced infringement of the seals of the sepulchre was made against the laws of honour and honesty. . . .
>
> In short, by the sealing of the stone of

the sepulchre we are to understand nothing less than a covenant entered into between our chief priests and the Apostles, by which Jesus' veracity, power, and Messiahship was to be try'd. . . .The condition of the sealed covenant was that if Jesus arose from the dead in the presence of our chief priests, upon their opening the seals of the sepulchre, at the time appointed; then he was to be acknowledged to be the Messiah. But if he continued in a corrupt and putrified state, then was he to be granted to be an impostor. Very wisely and rightly agreed! And if the Apostles had stood to this covenant, Christianity had been nipped in its bud and suppressed at its birth.

He anticipates the objection that the theft could not have escaped the notice of the soldiers set to guard the tomb. These were either bribed or, as " our ancestors said, what your evangelist has recorded," asleep.

The rabbi next raises the objection that Jesus appeared to none except the faithful:

Celsus of old, in the name of the Jews, made the objection, and Olivio, a later rabbi, has repeated it. But in all my reading and conversation with men or books I never met with a tolerable answer to it.
. . . This objection Origen owns to be a considerable one in his second book against Celsus.

Whoever blends together the various history of the four Evangelists as to Jesus' appearances after his resurrection will find himself not only perplex'd how to make an intelligible, consistent, and sensible story of it, but must, with Celsus, needs think it, if he closely think on 't, like some of the confused and incredible womanish fables of the apparitions of the ghosts of deceased persons, which the Christian world in particular has in former ages abounded with. The ghosts of the dead in this present age, and especially in this Protestant country, have ceased to appear; and we nowadays hardly ever hear of such an apparition. And what is the reason of it? Why, the belief of these stories being banish'd out of men's minds, the crafty and vaporous forbear to trump them upon us. There has been so much clear proof of the fraud in many of these stories that the wise and considerate part of mankind has rejected them all, excepting *this* of *Jesus*, which, to admiration, has stood its ground. . . .

I can't read the story without smiling, and there are two or three passages in it that put me in mind of *Robinson Crusoe's* filling his pockets with biskets, when he had neither coat, waistcoat, nor breeches on.

I don't expect my argument against it [the Resurrection] will be convincing of any of your preachers. They have a potent reason for their faith, which we *Jews* can't come at; or I don't know but we might believe with them.

That the Fathers, without questioning their belief of Jesus' corporal Resurrection, universally interpreted the story and every part of it mystically, is most certain.

He cites Hilary in behalf of this contention; also Augustine, *Sermo* clxviii., Appendix; Origen in *Johan. Evang.*, C. xx., Tract 120; John of Jerusalem, *In Matt.*, c. xx.; Jerome, *In Matthæum;* and then sums up his case in the following words:

What I have said in a few citations is enough to show that they looked upon the whole story as emblematical of his Spiritual Resurrection out of the *grave* of the *letter* of the Scriptures, in which he has been buried about *three days* and *three nights*, according to that mystical interpretation of prophetical Numbers which I have learned of them . . by the three Days, St. Augustine says, are to be understood three ages of the world.

I am resolved to give the Letter of the Scripture no rest, so long as God gives me life and abilities to attack it. Origen (in Psalm xxxvi.) says that, *when we dispute against Ministers of the Letter, we must select some historical parts of Scripture, which they understand literally, and show that, according to the Letter, they can't stand their ground, but imply absurdities and nonsense.* And how then is such a work to be performed to best advantage? Is it to be done in a grave, sedate, and serious manner? No, I think ridicule should here take place of sober reasoning, as the more proper and effectual means to cure men of their foolish faith and absurd notions.

I have cited Woolston's argument against the Resurrection so fully in order to give my readers an adequate idea of his method. It is old-fashioned, no doubt, as compared with the much subtler criticism of the Abbé Loisy, who challenges the story of the empty tomb altogether, and argues that, Jesus having been really cast after death into the common foss or Hakeldama into which other malefactors' bodies were thrown, the story of the women's visit to the empty tomb was invented to buttress the growing belief in a bodily resurrection, such as became a messiah who was to return and inaugurate an earthly millennium. As against the traditional acceptance of the narratives, however, Woolston's arguments are effective enough. His method of ridicule was, of course, adopted by Voltaire, who was living in England when he and Collins were writing. Voltaire, indeed, would have been the first to laugh at the method of allegory by which the two English Deists sought to quicken into spiritual meanings the letter which killeth by its absurdities. Needless to relate, this saving use of allegory did not avail to protect Woolston from public insults, prosecutions, and imprisonment. He was twice attacked by zealots in front of his house, and

was in the King's Bench tried before a jury who
found him guilty of blasphemy. He was fined
a hundred pounds, and, being unable to pay,
he went to prison for the last four years of his
life. The mere titles of the books written to
answer him sufficiently indicate the odium
they excited. Here are two of these titles:

> Tom of Bedlam's short letter to his
> cozen Tom Woolston, occasioned by his late
> discourses on the miracles of our Saviour.
> London, 1728.
> For God or the Devil, or just chastise-
> ment no persecution, being the Christian's
> cry to the legislature for exemplary punish-
> ment of publick and pernicious blasphemers,
> particularly that wretch Woolston, who has
> impudently and scurrilously turned the
> miracles of our Saviour into ridicule. Lon-
> don, 1728.

The question remains whether Collins and
Woolston were sincere in their advocacy of an
allegorical interpretation of the Bible. I feel
sure that Collins was, but not that Woolston
was so, at any rate in his latest works. The
worst of them were dedicated in insulting terms
to English bishops of note, whom he invariably
characterised as hireling priests and apostates.
For Whiston, who as a professed Arian was
hardly less offensive to the clergy than himself,
Woolston ever retained his respect, though, like

Collins, he forfeited his friendship. On the whole, there is much to be said for Leslie Stephen's verdict that the study of Origen or some similar cause had disordered his intellect. In other words, he was a religious crank.

However this be, there is one aspect of these two Deists which escaped their contemporaries and all who have since written about them. It is this, that in dismissing the historical reality of Christ's miracles in favour of an exclusively symbolic interpretation they exactly took up the attitude of the medieval Cathars, called sometimes Albigensians, sometimes Patarenes. Thus in an old imaginary dialogue of the twelfth or thirteenth century, written by a Catholic against these heretics, the Catholic asks: "Why, like Christ and the Apostles, do you not work visible signs?" And the Patarene answers:

> Even yet a veil is drawn in your hearts, if you believe that Christ and his apostles worked visible signs. The letter killeth, but the spirit quickeneth. Ye must therefore understand things in a spiritual sense, and not imagine that Christ caused the soul of Lazarus to return to his corpse; but only that, in converting him to his faith, he resuscitated one that was dead as a sinner is dead, and had lain four days, and so stunk in his desperate state.

These curious heretics, the descendants of

Marcion and Mani, held that, as matter was an evil creation, Christ, a spiritual and divine being, could not have wrought material miracles; he could not pollute himself by contact with matter. He only appeared to the eye to work material signs, just as he appeared to the eye to have a human body, though, in fact, he shared not our flesh and blood. His birth, therefore, no less than his death and resurrection, were only fantastic appearances, and not real events.

It is strange to find Woolston reproducing these earlier forms of opinion. Did he blunder into them by himself, or did he, through some obscure channel, inherit them? If we consider that these medieval heretics were in the direct pedigree of some of the Quaker and Anabaptist sects which in the seventeenth century swarmed in England, Holland, and Germany, it is not impossible that he picked up the idea from some of his contemporaries.

CHAPTER IV

The Evangelists

A LEADING writer of the Latin Church, the Rev. Joseph Rickaby, in an essay on "One Lord Jesus Christ," in a volume entitled *Jesus or Christ*, London, 1909, p. 139, has written as follows:

> At the outset of the argument it is necessary to define my controversial position in reference to the books of the New Testament. Never have documents been attacked with greater subtlety and vehemence: at the end of forty years' fighting they have emerged in the main victorious; their essential value has been proved as it never had been proved before.

That Dr. Rickaby is easily pleased will be seen if we consider the results of those forty years of criticism as they are accepted by a daily increasing number of clergymen in the Roman, Anglican, and Lutheran Churches, and also by many Nonconformists. In the first place, the gospel called "according to Matthew" is no longer allowed to be from the pen of that Apostle. Here again we may select Dean Alford as a fair representative of educated opinion fifty years ago. He could then write of the passage Matt., viii., 2 *ff.*, in which the cleansing of a leper by Jesus is related, as follows:

> This same miracle is related by St. Luke (ch. v., 12–14) without any mark of definiteness, either as to time or place. . . . The plain assertion of the account in the text requires that the leper should have met our Lord on his descent from the mountain, while great multitudes were following him. . . . I conceive it highly probable that St. Matthew was himself a hearer of the sermon (on the mount) and one of those who followed our Lord at this time.

And again, in reference to the passage ix., 9, where the publican called by Jesus to be an apostle is called Matthew, in contradiction of the other two gospels, which give his name as Levi, Alford could write that "it is probable enough that Matthew, in his own gospel, would mention only his apostolic name," and that "in this case, when he of all men must have been best informed, his own account is the least precise of the three." And in his Prolegomena, in ch. ii., he begins the section upon the authorship of this gospel with the words:

> The author of this gospel has been uni-

versally believed to be the Apostle Matthew. With this belief the contents of the gospel are not inconsistent, and we find it current in the very earliest ages.

Alford also believed that the three Synoptic Gospels substantially embody the testimony the Apostles gave of Christ's ministry, from his baptism by John until his ascension; that this testimony was chiefly collected from the oral teaching current among the catechists of the Church, but in part from written documents as well which reflected the teaching. He was furthermore convinced that no one "of the three evangelists had access to either of the two gospels in its present form.'" He was loth to believe that Matthew, an Apostle, was a debtor to either of the others, not only for the order in which he arranges the events of the ministry of Jesus, but also for great blocks of his texts. Yet that Matthew was so indebted to Mark is an axiom with modern orthodox critics. The first gospel is universally allowed to-day to be a compilation by an unknown writer of two ulterior documents—namely, Mark and the non-Marcan document already mentioned.[1]

In another work, *Myth, Magic, and Morals*, I have advised my readers to take a red pencil and underline in the Gospels of Matthew and Luke all the phrases, sentences, and entire narratives

[1] See page 25.

which agree verbally with Mark, so that they may realise for themselves how little of Mark is left that is not either in Matthew or in Luke. Or, conversely, they may underline in Mark all words or parts of words that are found in the other two gospels. In the latter case they will find that they have underlined almost the whole of Mark. The only explanation is that both the others used Mark; and accordingly Dr. Armitage Robinson, a fairly conservative critic, writes in his work on *The Study of the Gospels* as follows:

> I think that the impression gained by any one who will take the trouble to do what I have suggested (viz., underline common words, etc.) will certainly be that St. Mark's Gospel lay before the other two evangelists, and that they used it very freely, and between them embodied almost the whole of it.

Accordingly Dr. Robinson boldly asserts (p. 101) the first gospel to be the work of an *unknown* writer, and warns his readers to prefer either Luke or Mark or the reconstructed non-Marcan document to Matthew:

> From the historical point of view he cannot feel a like certainty in dealing with statements which are only attested by the unknown writer of the first gospel.

Here, then, we see a gospel that had all the

prestige of apostolic authorship, and the only one of the synoptics that had that prestige, debased to the level of an anonymous compilation, of less value for the historian than either of the other two. The one synoptic evangelist on whom Alford thought he could depend, just because he had seen things with his own eyes, turns out to be no apostle at all, but an anonymous copyist. Will Father Rickaby, in the face of such facts, continue to assert, of the first gospel at all events, that "its essential value has been proved as it never had been proved before"?

And in this connection it is instructive to note how the same hypothesis—viz., of Matthew's (and Luke's) dependence on Mark, and of Mark's priority—is regarded by two Anglican deans, respectively before and after its acceptance. A certain Mr. Smith, of Jordanhill, in a *Dissertation on the Origin and Connection of the Gospels* (Edinburgh, 1853), to which I shall return later, argued that oral tradition was not adequate to explain the identities of word and narrative which pervade the Synoptic Gospels; and he brought to a test the arguments on which the hypothesis of an oral tradition and narrative underlying them was based. That argument may fitly be given in the very words of Dean Alford, who believed in it. They are these (Prolegomena, ch. i., § 3, 6):

While they [the Apostles] were principally together, and instructing the converts
at Jerusalem, such narrative would naturally
be *for the most part the same*, and expressed
in the same, or nearly the same, words: coin-
cident, however, *not from design or rule*, but
because *the things themselves were the same;*
and the teaching naturally fell for the most
part into one form.

Mr. Smith brought this argument to the test
of experience by an examination of how far and
why modern historians like Suchet, Alison, and
Napier, narrating the same events, can approxi-
mate to one another. He proved that they only
agree verbally, as the Synoptic Gospels agree,
where they copied either one the other or all
common documents, and that where they did
not so copy they did not agree.

"Reasons could be assigned," answers Dean
Alford, "for the adoption or rejection by the
posterior writer of the words and clauses of the
prior one."   "Let the student," he continues,
"attempt such a rationale of any narrative common to the three gospels, on any hypothesis of
priority, and he will at once perceive its impracti-
cability. If Matthew, Mark, and Luke are to
be judged by the analogy of Suchet, Alison,
and Napier, the inference must be that, whereas
the historians were intelligent men, acting by
the rules of mental association and selection, the
evangelists were mere victims of caprice, and

such caprice as is hardly consistent with the possession of a sound mind."

This argument is unaffected by the circumstance that Matthew and Luke both copied Mark, instead of all three having (as was supposed by Mr. Smith) copied common, but now vanished, ulterior documents. What I desire to set on record is the condemnation Dean Alford is ready to mete out to Matthew and Luke in case they be proved to owe their mutual approximations, not to a common oral tradition, but to common documents. According to the present Dean of Westminster, that case was the real one. Dean Alford then, who was no mean scholar and exegete, admitted by anticipation that the first and third evangelists displayed an almost insane caprice in the handling of their sources. In adopting here and rejecting there the words and clauses of their sources they obeyed no rules of mental association or selection. In fine, Dean Alford, were he alive to-day, would have to condemn Matthew and Luke for the arbitrariness of their methods of compilation, in which he would discern no rhyme or reason. What, then, becomes of Dr. Rickaby's boast that after forty years' fighting his documents have emerged in the main victorious?

With Alford's judgment, however, let us contrast that of Dean Robinson, who, I believe, has always rejected that hypothesis of a common oral source, in which, like Alford, his master, Dr. Westcott acquiesced. He tells us that he entertained for a time the hypothesis of the use by all three evangelists of a common document, but finally dismissed it as "cumbersome and unnecessary, and adopted the view that the first and third embodied St. Mark in their respective gospels."[1] As to this "embodiment of St. Mark by the two subsequent writers," he holds that "it is not a slavish copying, but an intelligent and discriminating appropriation."

For myself, I am of opinion that the truth lies between Dean Alford and Dean Robinson. Matthew and Luke are indeed capricious in what they reject and what they adopt of Mark, but their caprice cannot be stigmatised as insane. It is only what we might expect of compilers who, living in uncritical and uncultivated circles, had no idea of using their sources in the careful and scrupulous manner in which a scientific historian of to-day would use them. Mark did not reach their hands as a canonical Scripture invested with authority; and in the view of one of them, Matthew, it was much more important that the events of Jesus' life should coincide with certain Messianic prophecies (as they were held to be) of the Old Testament than with the narrative of Mark. For

[1] See *The Study of the Gospels*, p. 28.

DR. WESTCOTT

73

several years I have occupied my spare time in comparing and sifting the narratives of the lives and martyrdoms of the Saints of the Church collected by the Jesuits in their vast series of volumes called the *Acta Sanctorum.* In these we can often trace the fortunes of an originally simple, naïve, and veracious narrative. Later hagiologists, intent on edification, pad out this narrative with commonplace miracles, stuff their own vulgar exhortations and admonitions in the mouths of the original actors, eliminate all local colour, and bowdlerise the text to suit a later stage of dogmatic development. Compared with such writers, it seems to me that Matthew and Luke treated the probably anonymous doctrines to which they owed their knowledge of Jesus with singular sobriety and self-restraint. We have only to compare either of them with the fourth Gospel to realise how much the art of portraying Jesus could decline in the course of little more than a generation.

Both Matthew and Luke had conceptions of the character and *rôle* of Jesus based partly on reflections of their own, partly on the growing prophetic gnosis of the age in obedience to which they remodelled Mark's narrative. Dean Robinson (in the work above mentioned) remarks that in Mark the emotions of anger, compassion, complacence, are each recorded of

Jesus three times; grief, agony, surprise, vehemence, each once. "Of actions," he continues, "we have 'looking around' five times, 'looking upon' twice, 'looking up' once, 'turning' thrice, 'groaning' twice, 'embracing in the arms' twice, 'falling down' once. Now, in the parallel passages of Matthew and Luke, we find," he says, "that all the more painful emotions disappear, with one exception (agony). Anger, grief, groaning, vehemence, are gone; compassion remains twice in St. Matthew, complacence (if it may be so termed) once in both."

Nor is it only in respect of Jesus that these "picturesque details" disappear. The figures of the disciples are purged in the same manner of human emotions. "Perplexity (five times), amazement (four), fear (four), anger (once), hardness of heart (once), drowsiness (once) are all recorded with more or less frequency in St. Mark. But in the other evangelists we find the same tendency to eliminate as before." It is very improbable that these later evangelists had an earlier copy of Mark from which these human traits in the portraiture of Jesus and his apostles were absent, waiting for the hand of a humanising editor to fill them in. Dean Robinson's explanation is much more likely, that this suppression of emotional attributes in the *personæ dramatis* was "the result of a kind of reverence which belonged to a slightly later stage of reflection, when certain traits might even seem to be derogatory to the dignity of the sacred character of Christ and his apostles.''

On the other hand, as Dean Robinson subtly remarks, the wonderment of the multitudes at the miracles of Jesus, already emphasised in Mark, is still further exaggerated in the later evangelists; and, as for the adversaries of Jesus, "we even seem to discover a general tendency both in St. Matthew and in St. Luke to expand and emphasise the notices of their hostility.''

This is the best sort of literary criticism, and it really marks an epoch in the history of the Christian religion in England when a Dean of Westminster can deliver it from his pulpit and publish it in a book. The only question is how far it tallies with his assertion that the two subsequent writers were intelligent and discriminating in their appropriation of Mark's narrative. Does it not rather show how swiftly the process was in progress of dehumanising Jesus, of converting him from a man of flesh and blood into a god, gifted with the *ataraxia* or exemption from human emotions proper to the Stoic ideal sage and king? This development culminates in the fourth Gospel. Pass from the defeated and tarnished, peevish and vindictive, prisoner of Elba to the majestic hero enthroned amid silence and awe in the spacious temple of the Invalides, and you feel that, *mutatis mutandis*, the cult of Napoleon between the years 1815 and 1850 presents a certain analogy with the deification of Jesus between the years A.D. 70 and 120.

Thus the early tradition that Matthew, as for sake of brevity I designate the first Gospel, was the work of an apostle and eye-witness has been definitely given up. It is possible that there may have been some truth in the tradition preserved by Papias about A.D. 120–140 that Matthew "composed the *logia* or oracles of the Lord in the Hebrew tongue—*i.e.*, in the Aramaic of Palestine, and that various people subsequently rendered these *logia* into Greek as best they could." Here we seem to get our only glimpse at the pre-Greek stage of the evangelical tradition, but we shall never know whether the word *logia* here used by Papias signified a collection of sayings or of narratives, or of both together. Many scholars to-day believe that Matthew's Hebrew *logia* were a selection of prophecies of Jesus Christ culled from the Old Testament. In any case our first Gospel is no translation of the document attested by Papias; for, as Dean Robinson remarks, "our St. Matthew is demonstrably composed in the main out of two Greek books," so that we must "conclude either that Papias made a mistake in saying that St. Matthew wrote in Hebrew, or that if he wrote in Hebrew his work has perished without leaving a trace behind it." There is further-more a statement in Irenæus (about 170–180) to the effect that Matthew published his Gospel among the Jews in his own tongue at the time that Peter and Paul were preaching the Gospel in Rome and founding the Church. This state-ment seems to be independent of that of Papias, as most certainly is the story related by Euse-bius of Pantænus, the catechist of Alexandria, and teacher of Clement and Origen. The story runs that about the year 180 Pantænus visited India and found the natives using a Gospel of Matthew written in Hebrew, which Bartholo-mew the Apostle had conveyed to them. Origen and Eusebius equally believed that our Matthew was the work of the Apostle, originally composed in Hebrew.

It surely denotes a great change, almost amounting to a revolution, when so ancient and well-attested a tradition as that which assigned the first Gospel to the Apostle Matthew is set aside by leaders of the English clergy; before long they must with equal candour abandon the yet more impossible tradition that the fourth Gospel was written by an Apostle and eye-witness John, the son of Zebedee, who in the Epistle to the Galatians is presented to us by Paul as a Judaiser and an ally of James, the brother of Jesus. The tradition that this Apostle wrote this Gospel is hardly so well authenticated as that which attested the apostolic origin of the first Gospel. It merely amounts to this, that as a child Irenæus had heard Polycarp, who died about A.D. 155, speak of John the Apostle. But he does not assert that Polycarp attributed the Gospel to the apostle, nor is the occurrence in a surviving letter of Polycarp to the Philippians of a phrase from the first Epistle of John proof that Polycarp either knew of the Gospel, or, if he knew of it, that he ascribed it to John any more than he does the epistle. It is, moreover, practically certain that the John of whom Irenæus in his boyhood heard Polycarp speak was not the apostle but the Presbyter John; for Irenæus reports that Papias, like Polycarp, was a disciple of this John, whereas Papias, according to the testimony of Eusebius, who had his works in his library, learned not from John the Apostle but from John the Presbyter much of what he recorded in the five books of his lost *Diégéseis*, or narratives. Irenæus, therefore, confused the two Johns. The external evidence of the existence of this Gospel is no doubt early and ample, but it is chiefly found among heretical and gnostic sects, like the Ophites, Perateans, Basilidians, and Valentinians; and one of the latter, Heracleon, wrote a commentary on it. The attribution to the Apostle John was probably made by some of these sects, just as the

Basilidians affected to have among them a
Gospel of Matthew, and as in other circles the
so-called Gospel of Peter was attributed to St.
Peter and read aloud in church as an authentic
work of that Apostle. If the fourth Gospel
took its origin from gnostic circles, we can quite
well understand why there existed so early in the
orthodox Church of Asia such strong prejudice
against it.

It is not long ago that Canon Liddon declared
in his Bampton Lectures (1866) that

> If the Book of Daniel has been recently
> described as the battlefield of the Old Testa-
> ment, it is not less true that St. John's Gos-
> pel is the battlefield of the New. It is well
> understood on all sides that no question of
> mere *dilettante* criticism is at stake when the
> authenticity of St. John's Gospel is chal-
> lenged. . . . For St. John's Gospel is the
> most conspicuous written attestation to the
> Godhead of Him whose claims upon man-
> kind can hardly be surveyed without passion,
> whether it be the passion of adoring love or
> the passion of vehement determined enmity.

Nevertheless, among the best educated Angli-
cans there is a tendency to give up the fourth
Gospel. In the work on the study of the
Gospels already commended[1] Dean Robinson
devotes two luminous chapters to the problem
of its age and authorship. Though he inclines

[1] See pp. 68 *ff.*

to accept it as a work written by the apostle in extreme old age, he is nevertheless not without sympathy for those who reject the orthodox tradition. "There are," he writes (p. 128), "many who are heartily devoted to that central truth [*i.e.*, of the divinity of Christ], but yet cannot easily persuade themselves that the fourth Gospel offers them history quite in the sense that the other Gospels do, cannot think that Christ spoke exactly as He is here represented as speaking, and consequently cannot feel assured that this is the record of an eyewitness, or, in other words, the writing of the apostle St. John."

It is worth while to cite some of the phrases in which Dr. Robinson describes the impression made by the first chapter of this Gospel (without going any further) on the mind of one who has steeped himself in the study of the three Synoptic Gospels:

> How remote do these theological statements (in the prologue of the fourth Gospel) appear from a Gospel narrative of the life of Christ, such as the three which we have been hitherto studying. . . .
> Our surprise is not lessened as we read on. Great abstract conceptions are presented in rapid succession: life, light, witness, flesh, glory, grace, truth.

Of the references to John the Baptist in chap. i.:

6

We are back on the earth indeed; but the scene is unfamiliar and the voices are strange. We hear not a word of John's preaching of repentance, or even of his baptism. This is no comment on the facts we know: it is a new story altogether. . . .

If a wholly new story of the beginnings of discipleship is offered us, this is not more startling than the wholly new story of John's disclaimer of Messiahship. . . .

Here, then, is a fair sample of the difficulty which this Gospel from beginning to end presents to those who come to it fresh from the study of the Synoptic narratives. The whole atmosphere seems different. . . .

Not only do the old characters appear in new situations—the scene, for example, being laid mostly in Jerusalem instead of Galilee—but the utterances of all the speakers seem to bear another impress. . . .

At times it is not possible to say whether the Lord Himself is speaking, or whether the evangelist is commenting on what He has said. The style and diction of speaker and narrator are indistinguishable, and they are notably different from the manner in which Christ speaks in the Synoptic Gospels. . . .

I do not, myself, see how a controversy of this kind can be closed. The contrast of which we have spoken cannot be removed; it is heightened rather than diminished as we follow it into details. . . .

Dean Robinson accepts, then, the tradition of apostolic authorship, but hardly on terms which leave to the Gospel more value as a record of the historical Jesus than the dialogues of Plato possess as a record of the historic Socrates. "It is," he avers, "not history in the lower sense of a contemporary narrative of events as they appeared to the youthful onlooker: not an exact reproduction of the very words spoken by Christ or to Christ."

And below he pictures the author of this Gospel as:

"An old man, disciplined by long labour and suffering, surrounded by devoted scholars, recording before he passes from them his final conception of the life of the Christ, as he looked back upon it in the light of fifty years of Christian experience. To expect that after such an interval his memory would reproduce the past with the exactness of despatches written at the time would be to postulate a miraculous interference with the ordinary laws which govern human memories.

The Christ is no longer "known after the flesh": the old limitations once transcended cannot be reimposed. A glorious vision results. A drama is enacted in which every incident tells, or it would not be there. The record moves not on the lines of the ordinary succession of events so much as on a pathway of ideas.

And once more he says of the author:

He can no longer sever between the fact

and the truth revealed by the fact: interpretation is blended with event. He knows that he has the mind of Christ. He will say what he now sees in the light of a life of discipleship.

For seventeen hundred years the theology which lifts Jesus of Nazareth out of and above human history, transforms him into the Word of God, which triumphed at Nicæa and inspired Athanasius, was based on this fourth Gospel more than on any other book of the New Testament. From it as from an armoury the partisans of the divinity of Jesus Christ, as the Church has understood and formulated that tenet in its creeds and councils, have constantly drawn their weapons. It now at last appears, by the admission of Dean Robinson, that this entire theological fabric was woven in the mind of an apostle meditating in extreme old age on the half-forgotten scenes and conversations of his youth. Such is the best case which can be made out for orthodox theology. We are left with the roofless ruins of the stately edifice which sheltered the orthodox doctors of the past. And even these ruins totter and seem to endanger the lives of the shivering, half-naked figures who seek a precarious shelter among them. Professor Sanday, who not long ago tried to save the apostolic authorship of the fourth Gospel by arguing that no one but an apostle would have ventured to handle with so much freedom the life and conversations of his Master, in his latest book gives signs of abandoning altogether the attribution to the son of Zebedee. The impression that Dean Robinson's pages leave on one's mind is that a real follower of Jesus could never have written such a gospel, though he himself scruples to draw the conclusion which his premisses warrant.

CHAPTER V

Textual Criticism

THE task of ascertaining the true text of a classical author, of Virgil or Tacitus, of Euripides or Lysias, is far simpler and less perplexed with problems than that of ascertaining the true text of an evangelist, or of any other New Testament writing. In the case of profane writers, we have merely to collate the manuscripts, to appraise their dates, to ascertain their mutual affinities, to draw out, if there be enough material, their genealogy, and discover which copies embody the oldest tradition; to detect and exclude the mechanical errors, the slips of the pen, of the scribe; to restore from the work of one copyist passages over which, because they began and ended with the same word or words, the eye of another copyist has glided, leaving a lacuna in his text. When all this is done there is room for conjectural emendators, the Porsons, Bentleys, Jebbs, Hermanns, to begin and exercise their ingenuity on passages that are evidently corrupt.

None of this labour can we spare ourselves in

the case of a sacred text, so-called; but much more awaits us besides. The profane author's work has never been the battle-ground of rival sects and creeds. No one ever asked Plato or Demosthenes to decide whether the miracle of the miraculous conception and birth really happened, whether God is a Trinity or no. They are no arbiters of orthodoxy, and carry no weight in the question of whether Mary was the mother of God or not, or whether the Son is consubstantial with the Father. It has been far otherwise with the Gospels and the rest of the New Testament ever since about the year 200. Until then Christians were so much possessed with the dream of the impending dissolution of all existing societies and institutions to make way for their own millennium, that they paid small attention to their scanty records of the earthly Christ, except so far as they were useful to confound their Jewish antagonists. Authority among them attached not to written documents, nor to priests and bishops, but to itinerant prophets, catechists, and ascetics. The composition of the Diatessaron,[1] about 180, was in itself no indication of excessive respect for the four Gospels conflated or fused together, but not harmonised, therein. If there had already then existed the same superstitious

---

[1] So called because it was a single Gospel produced by fusing together the four which still survive.

veneration for the four as was felt a hundred years later, Tatian would not have been permitted to make such a compilation of them, nor in Syria would his compilation have been accepted instead of the documents themselves as a manual to be publicly read in church. Probably at that time the individual Gospels were valued only as the Gospel of Mark and the non-Marcan document were valued by those who fused them together in our first and third Gospels; and few would have found fault with Tatian if he had re-arranged, curtailed, and otherwise modified his material on the same scale as these evangelists did theirs. The emergence of the several Gospels and their recognition about the year 200, alongside of the Old Testament, as authoritative Scriptures, unalterable and not to be added to, was the result of a gradual process; but the recognition, once effected, was all the more complete and absolute for having been so gradual. Probably when Irenæus, A.D. 180–200, pleaded that there could be only these four Gospels because there were only four winds, he was arguing against people who actually used other Gospels like that according to Peter and according to the Egyptians, and who regarded them, too, as sacred documents. From the little we know of these outside Gospels the Church did well to exclude them from its canon.

But to canonise a document is to expose it to many dangers, for every one wants to have it on his side. Luckily the great controversies of the Church began in the third century only, when the Gospel text was already too well fixed and settled for partisans to interfere with it on the large scale on which Marcion tampered with Luke. Nevertheless, there are signs that it was in details changed to suit new developments of doctrine, even at a very early period; and in my volume, *Myth, Magic, and Morals*, I have given several examples of such doctrinal alterations of the text. Of these examples one was the story of the rich youth who aspired to become a disciple. It is read in Matt. xix., 16, Mark x., 17, Luke xviii., 18. Dr. Salmon, of Dublin, availed himself of this passage in order to show how "close is the connection between the criticism of the Gospel text and theories concerning the genesis of the Gospels."[1] We can seldom estimate the originality and value of rival variants found in one Gospel without considering what is read in the other two, supposing these to contain parallel versions of a saying or incident. It is, for example, no use to argue, as did the Cambridge editors, Westcott and Hort (who shaped the Revised Version's text), that for Matthew the MSS. Aleph. B.D.L., on the

[1] George Salmon, *Some Criticism of the Text of the New Testament*, London, 1897, p. 117.

whole, give the sound and true tradition, and that their reading is, therefore, to be preferred in the passage in question. The other two Gospel texts, especially if looked at in the light of the modern theory of the interrelations of the three synoptics, assure us that those MSS. here contain what we may term an orthodox corruption.

The critic I have just quoted, the late Dr. Salmon, whose kindness to myself when I was a youthful scholar I shall not soon forget, expresses in the same context his conviction that the work of Westcott and Hort suffered much from their want of interest in the problem of the genesis of the Gospels. Westcott, in particular, seems never to have abandoned the very inadequate view which he propounded in 1860 in his *Introduction to the Study of the Gospels*, that their points of agreement and disagreement are to be explained from oral tradition alone. There was, he argues, a body of oral tradition existing and passing from teacher to taught in both an Aramaic and a Greek form. Mark wrote down the Greek tradition in its earliest form, then Luke wrote it down in a developed form, and the Greek Matthew wrote down the later Hebraic remoulding of the tradition; but no common document underlay either all three or any two of them. He admitted indeed that "No one at present [A.D. 1860] would maintain with some of the older scholars of the Reformation that the coincidences between the Gospels are due simply to the direct and independent action of the same Spirit upon the several writers." In other words, the common element in these Gospels was not the Holy Spirit. Yet that it might just as well be the Holy Spirit as a merely oral tradition will, I believe, be plain to any one who reflects how impossible it is that three independent writers should remember a long and complicated body of incident and teaching in the same way, and transfer it to paper, page after page, in almost identical words.

I will conclude this chapter by glancing at some famous orthodox corruptions, the history of which, as a lesson in the psychology of obstinacy, is hardly less instructive than the story of Dr. Bode's bust of Leonardo da Vinci's Flora.

In the First Epistle of John, chap. v., verse 7, most but not all copies of the Latin Bible, called the Vulgate, read as follows:

> For there are *three that bear witness in heaven: the Father, the Word, and the Holy Spirit; and these three are one. And* there are three that bear witness on earth: the Spirit and the water and the blood; and these three are one.

In the first printed edition of the New Testa-

ment, called the Complutensian, prepared at
Alcala in Spain in 1514 by Cardinal Francis
Ximenes, the words here italicised were included,
having been translated from the Latin text into
Greek; for the Greek MSS. used did not contain
them.   They are only found in two Greek MSS.,
one of the fifteenth, the other of the sixteenth century.   About 400 other Greek codices from the
fourth century down to the fourteenth ignore
them.   All MSS. of the old Latin version anterior
to Jerome lack them, and in the oldest copies
even of Jerome's recension of the Latin text,
called the Vulgate, they are conspicuously absent.
The first Church writer to cite the verse in such
a text was Priscillian, a Spaniard, who was also
the first heretic to be burned alive by the Church
in the year 385.   After him Vigilius, Bishop of
Thapsus, cites it about 484.   It is probable that
the later Latin Fathers mistook what was only a
comment of Cyprian, Bishop of Carthage (died
258) for a citation of the text.   In any case, it
filtered from them into the Vulgate text,[1] from
which, as we have seen, it was translated into
Greek and inserted in two or three very late
manuscripts.

[1] Gibbon, in a note on chap. xxxvii. of his *Decline and
Fall*, says that in the eleventh and twelfth centuries the
Bibles were corrected by Lanfranc, Archbishop of Canter-
bury, and by Nicolas, Cardinal and librarian of the
Roman Church, *secundum orthodoxam fidem*. (Wetstein,
Prolegom., pp. 84, 85.)

Erasmus's first edition of the Greek Testament, in 1516, omitted the verse, as also did the second; but in 1522 he issued a third edition containing it. Robert Stephens also inserted it in his edition of 1546, which formed the basis of all subsequent editions of the Greek Testament until recently, and is known as the Received Text, or *Textus Receptus.*[1]

In 1670 Sandius, an Arian, assailed the verse, as also did Simon, a learned Roman Catholic priest, in his *Histoire Critique du Nouveau Testament*, part i., chap. 18, about twenty years later. He was followed by Sir Isaac Newton, who, in a learned dissertation published after his death in 1754, strengthened Simon's arguments. Oddly enough, a Huguenot pastor, David Martin (1639–1721), of whom better things might have been expected, took up the cudgels in defence of the text. "It were to be wished," he wrote, "that this strange opinion had never quitted the Arians and Socinians; but we have the grief to see it pass from them to some Christians, who, though content to retain the doctrine of the Trinity, abandon this fine passage where that holy doctrine is so clearly taught." With the same tolerance of fraud, so long as it makes for orthodoxy, an Anglican bishop added a footnote in his catechism to the effect that the authenticity of this text, although

[1] See Chap. VIII.

by many disputed, must be strenuously upheld because it is so valuable a witness to the truth of Trinitarian doctrine. Gibbon, in his thirty-seventh chapter, sarcastically wrote:

> The memorable text which asserts the unity of the Three who bear witness in Heaven is condemned by the universal silence of the orthodox fathers, ancient versions, and authentic manuscripts. . . . After the invention of printing, the editors of the Greek Testament yielded to their own prejudices, or those of the times; and the pious fraud, which was embraced with equal zeal at Rome and Geneva, has been infinitely multiplied in every country and every language of modern Europe.

This passage provoked an attack on Gibbon from a certain English Archdeacon, Travis, who rushed into the arena to defend the text which Kettner, answering Simon nearly a century earlier, had extravagantly hailed as "the most precious of Biblical pearls, the fairest flower of the New Testament, the compendium by way of analogy of faith in the Trinity." It was high time that forgers should receive a rebuke, and Porson, the greatest of English Greek scholars and critics, resolved to administer it to them. In a series of *Letters to Travis* he detailed with merciless irony and infinite learning the history of this supposititious text. Travis answered that Porson was a Thersites, and that he despised his railings. He accused him of defending Gibbon, who, as an infidel, was no less Porson's enemy than his own. Porson's answer reveals the nobility of his character. "Why," he replies, "for that very reason I would defend him"—a retort worthy of Dr. Johnson.

Scarcely anything in the English language is so well worth reading as these letters of Porson, and I venture to quote from his preface a single passage about Bengel (died 1752), whose commentary on the New Testament called the Gnomon was, for its day, a model of learning and acumen:

> Bengel [writes Porson] allowed that the verse was in no genuine MS., that the Complutensian editors interpolated it from the Latin version, that the Codex Britannicus is good for nothing, that no ancient Greek writer cites it and many Latins omit, and that it was neither erased by the Arians nor absorbed by the homœoteleuton. Surely, then, the verse is spurious. No; this learned man finds out a way of escape. The passage was of so sublime and mysterious a nature that the *secret discipline* of the Church withdrew it from the public books, till it was gradually lost. Under what a want of evidence must a critic labour who resorts to such an argument.

Porson made himself unpopular by writing these

letters. The publisher of them lost money over the venture, and an old lady, Mrs. Turner, of Norwich, who had meant to leave him a fortune, cut down her bequest to thirty pounds, because her clergyman told her that Porson had assailed the Christian religion.

The revised English version of this passage omits, of course, the fictitious words, and gives no hint of the text which was once so popular. Archdeacon Travis is discreetly forgotten in the Anglican Church; but the truth has far from triumphed in the Roman, and Pope Leo XIII., in an encyclical of the year 1897, solemnly decreed that the fraudulent addition is part of authentic scripture. He was surrounded by reactionaries who imagined that, if they could wrest such a pronouncement from the infallible Pontiff, they would have made an end for ever of criticism in the Catholic Church. The abbot of Monte Casino, the home of the Benedictines, was, it is said, on the point of publishing a treatise in which he traced this forgery to its sources, when the Pope's decree was issued. He thrust back his treatise into his pigeon-holes, where it remains. The aged Pope, however, who was a stranger to such questions, soon realised that he had been imposed upon. Henceforth he refused to descend to particulars, or to condemn the many scholars delated to him as modernist heretics. Of these the Abbé Loisy

ALFRED LOISY.

97

was the chief, and the outcry against him finally
decided Leo to establish in 1902 a commission
for the progress of study of holy scripture.   For
the first time a few specialists were called in
by the head of the Catholic Church to guide
his judgment in such matters, and Leo XIII.
directed them to begin by studying the question
of the text, 1 John v., 8.   They presently sent
him their report.   As this was to the effect that
the text was not authentic, it was pigeon-holed.
But the aged prelate's mind was ill at ease; and
during his last illness, both in his lucid moments
and in delirium, he could talk of nothing else.[1]
He has been succeeded by one who has no
qualms, but condemns learning wherever and
whenever he meets with it.   To be learned in
that communion is in our age to be suspect.

There is a similar Trinitarian text in Matthew
xxviii., 19, where the risen Christ is represented
as appearing to his twelve apostles on a mountain top in Galilee and saying to them: *All
authority hath been given unto me in heaven and on
earth.   Go ye therefore, and make disciples of all
the nations, baptising them into the name of the
Father and of the Son and of the Holy Ghost;
teaching them to observe all things whatsoever I com-
manded you: and lo, I am with you alway, even
unto the end of the world.*

[1] I derive these statements from the Abbé Albert Houtin,
La Question Biblique au XXe Siècle.   Paris, 1906, p. 94.

Here Eusebius, Bishop of Cæsarea, who died about the year 340, and was entrusted by the Emperor Constantine with the task of preparing fifty *éditions de luxe* of the gospels for the great churches built or rebuilt after the Diocletian persecution was ended, read in such of his works as he wrote before the year 325 as follows: "Go ye therefore, and make disciples of all the nations *in my name;* teaching them," etc.

It is clear, therefore, that of the MSS. which Eusebius inherited from his predecessor, Pamphilus, at Cæsarea in Palestine, some at least preserved the original reading, in which there was no mention either of Baptism or of Father, Son, and Holy Ghost. It had been conjectured by Dr. Davidson, Dr. Martineau, by the present Dean of Westminster, and by Professor Harnack (to mention but a few names out of many), that here the received text could not contain the very words of Jesus—this long before any one except Dr. Burgon, who kept the discovery to himself, had noticed the Eusebian form of reading.

It is satisfactory to notice that Dr. Eberhard Nestle, in his new edition of the New Testament in Latin and Greek, furnishes the Eusebian reading in his critical apparatus, and that Dr. Sanday seems to lean to its acceptance. That Eusebius found it in his MSS. has been recently contested by Dr. Chase, the Bishop of Ely, who argues that Eusebius found the *Textus Receptus* in his manuscripts, but substituted the shorter formula in his works for fear of vulgarising and divulging the sacred Trinitarian formula. It is interesting to find a modern bishop reviving the very argument used 150 years ago in support of the forged text in 1 John v., 7. It is sufficient answer to point out that Eusebius's argument, when he cites the text, involves the text "in my name." For, he asks, "In whose name?" and answers that it was the name spoken of by Paul in his Epistle to the Philippians ii., 10. It is best to cite the entire passage, which is in the *Demonstratio Evangelica* (col. 240, p. 136 of Migne's edition):

> For he [Jesus] did not enjoin them to make disciples of all the nations simply and without qualification, but with the essential addition "in his name." For so great was the virtue attaching to his appellation that the Apostle says (Phil. ii., 10) "God bestowed on him the name above every name: that in the name of Jesus every knee shall bow, of things in heaven and earth and under the earth." It was right, therefore, that he should lay stress on the virtue of the power residing in his name, but hidden from the many, and therefore say to his apostles, "Go ye and make disciples of all the nations in my name."

Surely Dr. Chase would not argue that the name implied in Phil. ii., 10, was the name of

Father, Son, and Holy Spirit. That would be a pretty heresy for an Anglican bishop to entertain. Would he attribute a heresy at once so violent and senseless to Eusebius? Where, then, is the point of arguing that Eusebius, in the score of passages where he cites Matt. xxviii., 19, in the above form, was moved by the *disciplina arcani*, or fear of divulging Christian mysteries, from writing the formula out—the more so as it was on the lips of many of his contemporaries and had been published long before by Dionysius of Alexandria, Cyprian, Tertullian, and perhaps by Irenæus and Origen? Why did they, too, not hide the sacred formula? Moreover, why should Eusebius drop out the command to baptise? Surely the *disciplina arcani* does not explain his omission of that?

In the case just examined it is to be noticed that not a single MS. or ancient version has preserved to us the true reading. But that is not surprising, for, as Dr. C. R. Gregory, one of the greatest of our textual critics, reminds us, "The Greek MSS. of the text of the New Testament were often altered by scribes, who put into them the readings which were familiar to them, and which they held to be the right readings."[1]

These facts speak for themselves. Our Greek

[1] *Canon and Text of the New Testament*, T. and T. Clark, 1907, p. 424.

texts, not only of the Gospels, but of the Epistles as well, have been revised and interpolated by orthodox copyists. We can trace their perversions of the text in a few cases, with the aid of patristic citations and ancient versions. But there must remain many passages which have been so corrected, but where we cannot to-day expose the fraud. It was necessary to emphasise this point because Drs. Westcott and Hort used to aver that there is no evidence of merely doctrinal changes having been made in the text of the New Testament. This is just the opposite of the truth, and such distinguished scholars as Alfred Loisy, J. Wellhausen, Eberhard Nestle, Adolf Harnack, to mention only four names, do not scruple to recognise the fact. Here is a line of research which is only beginning to be worked.

CHAPTER VI

SOME PIONEERS

PROINDE liber esse volo, "Henceforth I mean to be free," wrote Luther when he broke with the Pope; and he had the merit at least of throwing off authority and asserting the right and duty of the individual believer to read the Bible for himself and interpret it without the help of a priest. "*With all due respect for the Fathers*," he said, "*I prefer the authority of Scripture*" (*Salvis reverentiis Patrum ego præfero auctoritatem Scripturæ*).[1] In making such pronouncements Luther builded better than he knew, and if we would realise how much we owe to him for the bold challenge he hurled at Papal authority, we have only to compare the treatment by the Pope Pius X. of the Modernists, whose chief offence is desire to understand the Bible, with the respect paid in the Lutheran Church to such men as Harnack, Von Soden, Preuschen, Violet, and in the Anglican to such scholars as

---

[1] See Farrar's *History of Interpretation*, p. 327.

Robertson Smith, Professor Driver, Professor Sanday, Professor Burkitt. All these men would, in the Roman Church of the last ten years, have had to suppress or swallow their opinions, or would have been hounded out of the Church with writs of excommunication amid the imprecations of the orthodox crowd.

One of the earliest German scholars that attempted to understand the Gospels and divest the figure of Jesus of the suit of stiff dogmatic buckram with which theologians had immemorially bound him was the poet and philosopher, Johann Gottfried Herder, who made his literary *début* in 1773 in a volume of essays, to which Goethe also contributed. He was a humanist, a student of the classics, and an enthusiastic reader of Shakespeare. It was the age of Frederick the Great and Voltaire, an age when in north Germany men were able to think and write freely. In his first essay in theological criticism, entitled *Letters on the Study of Theology*, he urged that the Bible must be read from a human point of view, and intuitively discerned the impossibility of harmonising the fourth Gospel with the Synoptics. Orthodox divines, like the late Dr. Hort, a hundred years later among ourselves were still pretending that this Gospel supplements, but not contradicts, the other three. You may write a life of Jesus, argued Herder, out of John, or out of the Synop-

LUTHER.
105

tics, but not out of both sources at once, for they are irreconcilable with each other. John he declared to have been written from the standpoint of Greek ideas, as a corrective to the Palestinian Gospel which the other three reflect. They represent Jesus as a Jewish Messiah, John as Saviour of the world; and the latter drops out of sight the demonology of the other three because its author, like Philo, regarded it all as so much Palestinian superstition.

Yet Herder did not reject miracles. He even accepted that of the raising of Lazarus from the dead, and argued that the earlier gospels passed it over in silence in order not to excite the wrath of the Jews against the humble family · in Bethany! This argument is not too absurd for Dean Farrar to repeat it a hundred years later in his *Life of Christ* (p. 511). The first evangelists would not record "a miracle which would have brought into dangerous prominence a man who was still living. . . . Even if this danger had ceased, it would have been obviously repulsive to the quiet family of Bethany to have · been made the focus of an intense and irreverent curiosity," etc. With regard to the interrelations of the Synoptics, Herder showed more acumen, and anticipated the latest critical positions. Mark, he wrote, is no abridgment, but a true and self-contained Gospel; and if Matthew and Luke contain other and more

JOHANN GOTTFRIED HERDER.

matter, that is because they added it, and not because Mark, having it before him, left it out. Mark is the unadorned central column on which the other two lean—shorter than they, but more original. They added the Birth Stories because a new want of such information had, later than Mark, grown up among believers. And Mark indulges in less invective than they against the Jews, because the new religion was still largely a Jewish business. That neither the first three Gospels nor the fourth were intended to be read as sober historical treatises was also clear to Herder. The former were aimed to exalt him as a Messiah who fulfilled the Jewish prophecies; the fourth is an epic of the Logos.

But Herder's appreciations of the Life of Jesus were after all less scientific and earlier in type than those of Hermann Samuel Reimarus, of whose epoch-making contribution to the cause of New Testament criticism Albert Schweitzer has recently, in his work, *Von Reimarus zu Wrede*,[1] reminded those who had forgotten the great theological controversies of Lessing and Strauss. Reimarus, born in 1694,

---

[1] *From R. to W.*, Tübingen, 1906, lately issued in an English translation under the title *The Quest of the Historical Jesus*. On Reimarus and Lessing see also Scherer's *History of German Literature*, translated by Mrs. F. C. Conybeare, 1886, vol. ii., p. 72 *ff*.

was for forty-one years Professor of Philosophy in Hamburg, and died in 1768. He was the son-in-law of the famous philologist, J. Alb. Fabricius, and was himself a man of high classical attainments. He thus brought to the study of the New Testament a trained judgment, unspoiled by the narrow calling of the professional divine. His treatises on early Christianity were probably the more untrammelled by orthodox prejudices because they were not intended by him for publication, and they would never have seen the light had they not fallen into the hands of Lessing, who published in the years 1774–8 the more important of them under the title of *Fragments of an Anonymous Wolfenbütteler*. The German world had seemed to be in a mood for liberal criticism, and historians and humanists there, as in England, were already turning their attention to dogmatic religion; nevertheless, the Fragments fell like bombshells in the circles of the pious, and precipitated a real crisis in the history of the Protestant Church. The Christ of dogma was now arraigned as never before, and has, so to speak, been on trial ever since at the bar of History. For the fanciful figure of orthodox theologians the real historical Jewish Messiah began to emerge.

The message or Gospel of Jesus was, according to Reimarus, summed up in the appeal to his countrymen to repent, because the Kingdom

of Heaven was at hand.   But of the Kingdom he,
equally with John the Baptist, conceived in the
current Jewish manner; and if he transcended
his contemporaries in his forecast thereof, it
was only in so far as he taught that observance
of the Law of Moses would develop therein unto
a higher and deeper righteousness, less bound up
with sacrificial cult, false Sabbatarianism, and
ritual purity of meats.   He never broke with
the law nor dreamed of doing so.   It was only
when they were persecuted and driven out of
the synagogue that his disciples broke with it—
not of choice, but of necessity.

Thus the creed of the earliest Church consisted of the single clause: "I believe that Jesus
shall shortly inaugurate the Kingdom of God on
earth."   No   wonder   that   the   faith   spread
rapidly.   Multitudes were already filled with a
belief in the imminence of the promised Kingdom, and were but too ready to acclaim Jesus
as God's prophet and instrument in bringing it
about.   This was the whole of the message that
his apostles had to carry to the cities of Israel,
avoiding those of the Samaritans and Gentiles.
The Jews of Palestine were groaning under the
Roman yoke, and were prepared to welcome a
redeemer.   For them a Messiah was Son of God;
all the successors of David and kings of the
people of the Covenant were sons of God, but
the Messiah was such in a special sense.   The

Messianic claims of Jesus did not lift him above humanity, and there was nothing metaphysical about the *rôle*.

The Gospel parables teach us little of what the Kingdom was to be. They all assume that we know it. If we desire to learn more about it, we must go to the writings of the Jews. In any case the first condition of our understanding who and what Jesus was is that we should turn our backs on the catechism notions of a metaphysical sonship of God, of the Trinity, on orthodox dogmas in general, and should study instead current Jewish ideas. With these *a priori* notions will vanish the mistaken supposition that Jesus meant to found a new religion. He never dreamed of abolishing the Jewish religion and of substituting a new system in its place. His chief disciple, Peter, long after the resurrection, needed the vision at Joppa to assure him that he might without sin eat with men uncircumcised, and the disciples who fled from Jerusalem after Stephen's martyrdom "spoke the word to none save only to Jews." It follows that the text Matthew xxviii., 19 is impossible, not only because it is spoken by one risen from the dead, but because its tenor is universalist and it presupposes the Trinity and the metaphysical sonship of Jesus. It also conflicts with our earliest tradition of baptism in the community of Christians, for, as we learn both

from the Book of Acts and from Paul, they
baptised at first, not into the name of the three
Persons, but into that of Jesus the Messiah or
Christ.   Neither baptism nor in its later forms
the Eucharist derives from Jesus.

That Jesus worked cures which the people
round him regarded as signs and wonders cannot
be disputed.   When Reimarus further opines
that Jesus bade those he healed to tell no man
of it by way of exciting the curiosity of the
crowd, we cannot follow him.   But all will admit
that some of his greater miracles were invented
by propagandists who felt a call to prove that
in works of power the Messiah transcended the
worthies of the Old Testament.   If it be true
that in Jerusalem the multitude were as convinced as the texts assure us they were of his
immediately manifesting the Kingdom of God
to them, then by a single miracle publicly worked
on a feast-day he must have carried all before
him.   Twice he seems to have made sure that
his vision of the Kingdom was about to be
made a reality: once when, sending forth
his disciples, in Matt. x. 23, he coupled their
mission with the assurance that they would not
have time to visit all the cities of Israel before
the Son of Man came—that is, that the masses
flocking to him would erewhile have witnessed
the Messiah's advent; and a second time when,
in the style of Messiah, he entered Jerusalem

riding on an ass amid the acclamations of the multitude. But the people hung back after all, and his feat of clearing the temple of its Paschatide traffic fell flat, as also did his denunciations of priests and pharisees. The Galileans had forsaken him, and now the erewhile enthusiastic people of Jerusalem forsook him in the same way. He had begun by concealing his quality of Messiah of set purpose; he ended by concealing it from fear and necessity. He felt that his star had set and his mission was a failure when from the cross he uttered the bitter cry of disillusionment: "My God, my God, why hast thou forsaken me?" He had never contemplated suffering thus, never looked forward to a death on the cross. With God's miraculous aid he had expected to establish a kingdom on earth in which the Jews, rescued from the yoke of infidel and Gentile oppressors, would live happily ever afterwards; and now his countrymen betrayed and forsook him, and the Roman was slaying him with every circumstance of cruelty and mockery.

Reimarus shows less insight in his account of the events which followed the death of Jesus. He is right, no doubt, in arguing that the disciples, driven out of their old enthusiasms by the logic of facts, took refuge in Daniel's vision of an apocalyptic Son of Man, borne in glory on the clouds of heaven to earth. But when he gives credit to the story that the apostles stole the body of Jesus in order to accredit their story of his resurrection he betrays a certain want of grip. It was this feature of his reconstruction which more than any other roused against Lessing the accusation of impiety from those who for hundreds of years had complacently accepted Jerome's view that Peter and Paul had only got up their quarrel at Antioch for the gallery, and had never really been at issue with one another—a view that shocked even Augustine.[1]

Reimarus awoke many out of the torpor of assurance. Particular features of his system were no doubt erroneous, but in the main his arguments were irrefragable, because he interpreted his documents in their plain and literal, but to the orthodox disconcerting, sense. Modern criticism, even in Anglican and Roman circles, is slowly coming round to his chief conclusions, which were that Jesus never meant to found a new religion, but only to herald that Kingdom of God towards which the aspirations of pious Jews had for generations been directed, and that the fourth Gospel must simply be set

---

[1] See Jerome's 89th Epistle to Augustine, where he adheres to his view that Paul and Peter were both acting a part, and that they merely got up their tiff in order to reassure the Judaisers. Jerome argues that Paul was guilty of similar dissimulation when he took Timothy, a Gentile, and circumcised him for fear of the Jews.

aside by those who would discover the true Jesus. His account of Jesus' attitude towards the law, and of the gradual abandonment after his death of that attitude by his disciples, anticipated the best criticism of our own generation. When writers like Dean Farrar dilate on the "crude negations" and "dreary illuminism" of Reimarus,[1] they only betray their elementary ignorance of the problems they profess to solve.

About the same time as Reimarus was writing, a striking book appeared in England. This was E. Evanson's work on *The Dissonance of the Four Generally Received Evangelists and the Evidence of their Respective Authenticity Examined*. The author was born at Warrington, in Lancashire, in 1731, and received a classical education, first from his uncle, Mr. John Evanson, rector of Mitcham, in Surrey, and then at Emanuel, Cambridge. He graduated M.A. in 1753, took orders, and became his uncle's curate. But he was soon convinced that the prayer-book was opposed to Scripture, and accordingly omitted some phrases of it and changed others in public service. Having also maintained that Paul denied the physical as opposed to spiritual resurrection, he incurred a prosecution for heresy. The Solicitor-General, Mr. Wedderburn, defended him gratis on this occasion, and, having

[1] See Farrar's *History of Interpretation*, p. 400.

secured his acquittal, procured him Church preferment, not aware that Evanson had made up his mind to quit the Church.

It was supposed in 1772 that the Archbishop of Canterbury, with the help of certain of his colleagues, was preparing a revision of the Anglican liturgy and articles, so Evanson was encouraged to lay his scruples before him in a letter, in which he begged him to persevere, to remove difficulties, and ease the tender consciences of many learned clergymen. His extremely reasonable application was never answered, any more than has been the memorandum of nearly 2000 incumbents who recently approached the bishops in a similar spirit and with a like object. Mr. Evanson next published a letter to Hurd, Bishop of Lichfield, setting forth the grounds and reasons of his dissatisfaction, and shortly after left the Church, resigning his living. Hurd, in answer, expressed more regret than surprise, but praised him warmly for following his convictions. He only lamented the loss to the Church of one so full of liberal spirit and erudition. The Bishop of Rochester also expressed his concern that a clergyman of Mr. Evanson's abilities should resign his preferment for *no other reasons* than those he had assigned to the Bishop of Lichfield. Subsequently Evanson received a pension from the family of the Earl of Bute. "An open declaration of his faith, which duty called for and sincerity enjoined, provoked the rancour and malice of bigots and brought on him their hatred and persecution."[1] And certainly Mr. Evanson, at the outset of his work on the dissonances of the evangelists, strikes no uncertain note, for he begins as follows:

> After so many writers, some of them of great erudition and distinguished abilities, in almost all ages of what is called the Christian Church, have undertaken to harmonise and show the perfect agreement of the four generally received Evangelists, and to reconcile all the recurring differences in both the facts and order of their several narrations, it will undoubtedly appear the highest degree of presumptuous arrogance to attempt now at last to demonstrate that so much learned and ingenious labour hath been bestowed in vain.

Evanson gives examples of such dissonance both between one gospel and another, and between separate parts of the same gospel; but he made the mistake of overestimating the trustworthiness of Luke. This he was led to do because he was imposed on, firstly by the parade of historical method and research in

[1] From *Some Account of His Life and Religious Opinions*, written by a friend on the occasion of Evanson's death in 1805.

Luke's exordium, and secondly by Luke's excellence as a stylist. The latter quality particularly appealed to so refined a scholar. To illustrate this point I venture to cite his remarks about the passage, Matthew viii. 5–16 = Luke vii. 1–10, in which the healing of the Centurion's child is related. He notes that in Matthew the Centurion himself goes to Jesus, whereas in Luke he only sent a deputation of elders of the Jews, and declared that he did not esteem himself worthy to go in person. "Here, again," comments Evanson,

> one of these historians related a falsehood. It is observable also that, according to this gospel called St. Matthew's, this miracle, in order of time, preceded the healing of Peter's mother-in-law, the calling of Matthew himself, and the choice of the twelve apostles; whereas St. Luke tells us that it was subsequent to all three. Yet St. Luke assures Theophilus that, having attained perfect information of everything from the very first, he had written an account of every transaction *in order.* Now, he could have received his information only from the Apostles he lived with at Jerusalem, of whom Matthew was one; and as it is impossible but Matthew must have known whether he was himself with Jesus when this miracle was wrought or not, he could not have written that he was not and have informed St. Luke that he was; and, therefore, the writer of this

gospel could not be St. Matthew nor any other of the Apostles. To avoid unnecessary repetitions, the reader is desired to consider this as a general remark upon the many instances of contradiction, in the order of the narration, between this writer and St. Luke, which are both numerous and obvious to the least degree of attention.

Evanson also was shrewd enough to see that the legend of the miraculous birth of Jesus was no part of the primitive gospel tradition. He argues that the first two chapters of Luke are an interpolation; but he was well aware of the similarity of vocabulary and idiom which connects them with the rest of the gospel, and met this obstacle to his argument by supposing that the interpolator imitated Luke. He could not believe that the same hand which penned these two chapters could have narrated the incident of John sending his disciples to Jesus to ascertain if he was the Messiah. He writes thus:

Now, it seems absolutely impossible that John, after being from his earliest infancy personally acquainted with Jesus, and not only in possession of all the information respecting him, which he must have learned from the two families, but so miraculously impressed with affection and reverence for him as to exult with joy, though but an embryo in the womb, at the mere sound of his mother's voice, could at any time have entertained the least doubt of Jesus being the Messiah (p. 37).

The true view, of course, is that Luke, in spite of his pretensions to accuracy, was a careless and credulous writer.

Evanson's appreciations of the legend of the miraculous birth are couched in a very modern spirit. He notes that, according to Paul's preaching at Antioch, it was the resurrection and no birth miracle that constituted Jesus the Son of God; and also that Luke, except in his first two chapters, nowhere calls Jesus the Son of God until after the Resurrection. Before that event he terms him Son of Man or Son of David. On p. 44 he speaks of "this pagan fable of the miraculous conception of Jesus Christ"; and just below he writes on p. 49 as follows:

> In no one apostolic Epistle, in no one discourse recorded in the Acts of the Apostles, is the miraculous conception, or any circumstance of the history of Jesus previous to John's baptism, hinted at even in the most distant manner—on the contrary, that baptism is repeatedly referred to and mentioned as the proper commencement of evangelical instruction; and when the eleven Apostles proceeded to elect a twelfth, to supply the place of Judas, the only qualification made essentially requisite in the candidates was their having been eye-witnesses of our Lord's ministry from the baptism of

John to his Ascension. These two chapters of Luke are the daring fiction of some of the *easy-working* interpolators (ῥᾳδιουργόι), as Origen calls them, of the beginning of the second century, from among the pagan converts, who, to do honour as they deemed it to the author of their newly-embraced religion, were willing that his birth should, at least, equal that of the pagan heroes and demigods, Bacchus and Hercules, in its wonderful circumstances and high descent; and thereby laid the foundation of the succeeding orthodox deification of the man Jesus, which, in degree of blasphemous absurdity, exceeds even the gross fables of pagan superstition.

And in another place (p. 14) he remarks on the fact that Justin Martyr, in his *Apology*,

illustrates and pleads for the toleration of the orthodox doctrine of the generation of the Word by the heathen Emperors, because of its resemblance to the fabulous origin of their own deities Mercury and Minerva; and justifies the doctrine of the *incarnation* by its similarity to the births of Æsculapius and Hercules, and the other illustrious *god-men* of pagan mythology.

In these and many other passages Evanson belonged rather to the late nineteenth century than to the eighteenth. No one in his day realised so clearly as he the low standard, or no standard, of literary authenticity which charac-

terised early Christianity. Thus he notes that
in the earliest age it was so common among the
Christians "to produce entire pieces of their
own or others' forgery under the name of any
writer they pleased that, if what we call the
scriptures of the New Testament were not so
tampered with, they are almost the only writings,
upon the same subject, of those early times which
have escaped free."

It is a matter of common observation that,
in proportion as men overtop their contemporaries in one particular, they often lag behind
them in another; and a critic may see with one
eye and be blind of its fellow. It was so with
Evanson, who fell into the extraordinary error
of attaching to so-called prophecies of Christ an
importance which he denied to miracles. "Prophecy," he wrote, "is not only the most satisfactory, but also the most lasting, supernatural
evidence of the truth of any revelation." And
he even went the length of predicting from the
Apocalypse the end of the world within a few
generations. Just in proportion as he saw
clearly how insufficient is the evidence of the
gospels to bear the strain of the vast super-
structures that theologians have built upon them,
his mind seems to have been fuddled by the
study of this book. We have already seen that
Woolston was infected with the same craze; and
the great Isaac Newton himself, in the prime of

his life, gave up what time he could spare from his amazing mathematical and astronomical investigations to what, to a modern mind, are the silliest lucubrations about the vaticinations of the book of Daniel and of the Apocalypse.

In Joseph Priestley, born near Leeds in 1733, we have another example of a great man of science who was also a bold innovator in the domain of Church history. In early youth, he tells us, he "came to embrace what is generally called the heterodox side of every question." A *History of the Corruptions of Christianity*, published in 1782, and a *History of Early Opinions Concerning Jesus Christ*, printed in 1786, involved him in a long and keen controversy with an orthodox divine, Dr. Horsley. This divine was rewarded with a fat bishopric for detecting a few errors of scholarship in Priestley's works, while the latter a few years later, in 1791, was rewarded by having his house in Birmingham wrecked and set on fire by the Tory mob. The chemical instruments, by use of which he had carried on his epoch-making researches into the composition of gases and made his discovery of oxygen, were destroyed, his manuscripts torn to bits, and his books scattered for half-a-mile along the roadside. Priestley and his family barely escaped with their lives. His main heresy was the entirely correct opinion that the earliest Christians neither knew anything of Trinitarian doctrine nor deified Jesus after the manner of Athanasian doctrine. He denied. that the Apostles could have discerned God Almighty in the man of flesh and blood with whom they familiarly consorted. "I am really astonished," he wrote to Horsley, "how you can really entertain the idea of any number of persons being on this *even footing*, as you call it, with a being whom they actually believed to be maker of themselves and all things, even the Eternal God himself."[1] But Priestley did not question the authenticity of the writings of the New Testament any more than his master Socinus, and, like other Unitarians of that age, he accepted with implicit faith all the miraculous legends of the gospels except that of the Virgin birth. Within a charmed circle he shrank from applying his own canons of criticism. Leslie Stephen[2] remarks of Priestley that "it is still rather difficult to understand how so versatile and daring a thinker could have retained so much of the old system." But the same inconsistency reveals itself in numberless scholars of our own generation. Bishop Stubbs was the acutest of historical critics in the domain of general history, but to the Bible and to early Church history he brought the prejudices of a fourteenth-century monk; so also the modern

[1] Tracts, p. 259.
[2] *English Thought in the Eighteenth Century*, chap. vii., §6.

Bollandist editors of the Acts of the Saints, who are Jesuits, handle any legend later than the year 100 with the greatest freedom, yet abstain from applying the same rules and methods of historical investigation to the solution and sifting out of earlier Christian problems and narratives. The same remark holds good of the Abbé Duchesne, and of the late Bishop Creighton—not to mention countless scholars who really seem intent on running with the hare and hunting with the hounds at one and the same time.

Priestley also undertook to answer Evanson's arguments in a work which contains many suggestive passages. For example, he points out that

> the books called the Gospels were not the cause, but the effect, of the belief of Christianity in the first ages. For Christianity had been propagated with great success long before those books were written; nor had the publication of them any particular effect in adding to the number of Christian converts. Christians received the books because they knew beforehand that the contents of them were true (p. 8).

The last of these statements requires, no doubt, a little modification; but the entire passage suggests a fertile method of inquiry. Emerging in the bosom of an already long-established

Christianity, the Gospels could not fail in a large degree to reflect the sentiments, beliefs, prejudices, ritual practices, which arose in measure as the Faith spread among the Gentiles, was persecuted alike by Jews and Roman Government, was coloured by Greek philosophy, was divorced almost wholly from the scenes of its birth. This is how the Abbé Loisy envisages the whole problem of criticism of the New Testament. It is inseparable from an investigation of the circles of believers, called Churches, within whose medium the Gospels were produced and preserved. We have to determine how much of the record was primitive by separating from it all accretions due to this medium. If, therefore, Priestley had followed up this line of argument, he might have anticipated modern criticism. But he was, as we have said, a mixture of enlightenment and superstition. He could express himself "greatly obliged" to Evanson for the latter's "several new and valuable arguments against the miraculous conception," yet he accepted the fable of Balaam's ass, and failed to appreciate Evanson's argument that in the thirty years or more which by common consent elapsed between Jesus' ministry and the emergence of the earliest evangelical document there was ample time for the other miraculous stories of Jesus to have arisen in so credulous a medium as the early Church.

CHAPTER VII

Foreign Work

NO work recently published in Germany has made a greater stir in England than Albert Schweitzer's *Von Reimarus zu Wrede*, a systematic *résumé* and criticism of European study of the Gospels during the last hundred years. It is mortifying to us Englishmen to find that barely one page in a hundred of this remarkable book is devoted to works written by ourselves. The Germans, and in a measure the French, have for the last hundred years been making serious efforts to ascertain the truth about Christian origins. Our own divines, amid the contentment and leisure of rich livings and deaneries, and with the libraries and endowments of Oxford and Cambridge at their disposal, have done nothing except produce a handful of apologetic, insincere, and worthless volumes. The only books which in England have advanced knowledge have been translations of German or French authors, and not long since our well-endowed professors and doctors of divinity

127

greeted every fresh accession to Christian learning—when they could not ignore it and maintain
a conspiracy of silence—with dismal howls of
execration and torrents of abuse.   To three of
these foreign scholars, whose works in English
translations were so received, we must now turn.
They were David Friedrich Strauss, Ferdinand
Christian Baur (both Germans), and Ernest
Renan, a Frenchman.

Of these the second was the oldest; he was
born in 1792, and died in 1860.   The son of a
Würtemberg clergyman, he was still further
attracted to theological study by the influence
of Bengel, his uncle, the scholarly, but orthodox,
leader of the theological school in the University
of Tübingen towards the close of the eighteenth
century.   He was first a pupil and then a teacher
at the Blaubeuren Seminary, where he numbered
Strauss among his pupils.   Thence he was, in
1826, promoted to a professorship at Tübingen
in succession to Bengel.   His geniality and
freedom from affectation and pedantry, combined with a noble presence, were enough in
themselves to attract young men to his courses;
but the ring of sincerity, the underglow of
devotion to truth, drew to him the affection of
all the finer natures among them.   He inspired
hundreds with his own zeal and ardour for
learning, his bold impartiality in pursuit of truth,
and without conscious effort he thus created

F. C. Baur.

what was known as the Tübingen school, still
the bogie of English clergymen when I was myself
a youth in the years 1875–1890.   In this school
were formed such scholars as E. Zeller (Baur's
son-in-law), K. R. Köstlin, Adolf Hilgenfeld of
Jena, Otto Pfleiderer of Berlin, Gustav Volkmar
of Zürich (died 1896), Edmond Scherer and
Timothée Colani in France, the founders of the
Revue de Théologie.

Baur discerned a key to the understanding
of early Church history in the antagonism between Paul and his school on the one side, who
desired the free admission of uncircumcised
Gentiles into the Messianic society which
gathered around the memory of Jesus, and Peter
and John, his personal disciples, and James, his
brother, and first president of the Church of
Jerusalem, on the other.   The latter had known
Jesus in the flesh, and insisted on the observance
of the Jewish law in the matter of food and
meats, ablutions, Sabbath observance, and
circumcision.   They would have confined the
new "heresy" or following of Jesus Christ to
Jews and orthodox proselytes.   Through the
gate of the old law alone could any enter the
promised Kingdom which a *deus ex machina* was
soon to substitute on Jewish soil for the dis-
graceful tyranny of a Roman governor and his
legions.   This antagonism colours the four
great epistles of Paul, Romans, 1 and 2 Corin-

thians, and Galatians, and the hatred of Paul long continued among the Palestinian Christians, who caricatured him as Simon Magus, and adopted the lifelike personal description of him which still survives in the "Acts of Thekla" as a picture of the Anti-Christ.

This antagonism between Peter and Paul, the two traditional founders of the leading Church of Rome, was for the Catholic Church a sort of skeleton in the cupboard, and caused much searching of hearts among the orthodox as early as the fourth century. By way of setting their misgivings at rest, Jerome advanced his famous hypothesis that the dispute with Peter related by Paul in the Epistle to the Galatians was no more than a comedy arranged between the two in order to throw Jewish zealots off the scent. In general, orthodox historians have sought to minimise the importance of the matter; they could hardly do otherwise. But Baur was not a man to wriggle out of a difficulty. He saw, and rightly saw, its importance; and he tried to reconstruct the chronological order of the earliest writings of the Church on the principle that those in which the quarrel is still open and avowed must have preceded those which try to gloss it over and to pretend that it was never serious. In proportion, Baur argued, as the antagonism died down and leading men on each side drew together in the face of persecution by

Jews and Romans, and of the disintegrating
propaganda of the Gnostics, the Catholic
Church emerged, a middle party, which little
by little absorbed the extremes, and whose
literature was largely inspired by the wish to
conceal even the scars of wounds which had once
bled so freely.   In the four epistles of Paul above
named the quarrel is still fresh and actual, and
therefore they are the most primitive documents
we have, and are prior to the year 70.   So is
the Apocalypse, an Ebionite document breathing hatred of Paul.   The Synoptic Gospels and
Acts were written in the interests of reconciliation, and followed, instead of preceding, the lost
gospels of Peter, of the Hebrews, of the Ebionites,
of the Egyptians.   They are the literary pre-
cipitate of oral tradition going back in certain
particulars to the Apostolic age, but, as documents, hardly earlier than the middle of the
second century.   The Gospel of Matthew is the
earliest of them, and most Ebionite; then came
that of Luke, of which the elements took shape
under Pauline influence.   It is an amplification
of Marcion's Gospel.   Last is Mark's, a neutral
gospel, made up of odds and ends from the
other two.   The rest of the Pauline epistles are,
all of them, reconciliation documents of about
the middle of the second century.   The book
called Acts is an irenicon penned to show how
harmoniously Peter and Paul could work to-

gether, and what good friends they were. The epistles of Peter were literary forgeries designed with the same object, and the Fourth Gospel and the Epistles of John are later than 160.

The fault of Baur was that he worked his theory for more than it was worth; that he failed to give due weight to many other ideas and tendencies which equally influenced the development of Church opinion and literature; and, lastly, that he set nearly all the documents at least fifty years too late. Later research has triumphantly proved that Mark is not a compilation from Matthew and Luke, but their basis, and that our Luke was in Marcion's hands, and mutilated by him to suit his views. Large fragments of the Gospel of Peter, and, probably, of that of the Egyptians, have been rescued from the tombs and sands of Egypt; and it turns out that, even if they were not copied or imitated from the Synoptics, they were certainly not their sources. Generally speaking, they are more modern in their tone and post-Galilean. A more thorough examination of the idiom and vocabulary of 1 Thessalonians, Philippians, and Philemon shows that these epistles are from the same hand which penned the four undisputed ones; and Baur's greatest disciple, Hilgenfeld, has shown this to be the case. One great merit, however, must anyhow be ascribed to Baur, that of forcing all subsequent

investigators to consider the documents purely
in relation to the age which saw their birth, and
to explain them from the influences which were
at work, instead of envisaging them as isolated
works of detached thinkers and teachers.   If a
book seems to be a forgery, we must at once ask
Cui bono—in the interests of what and of whom
was it forged?   If it is admittedly authentic, its
place in the development of doctrine and opinion
and events, the phase which it reflects, must
still be studied and set forth.   Historical perspective is all-important, no less in relation to
the documents of the early Church than to those
of any other literature.   This must ever be the
most fruitful method of interpretation, and it is
a hopeful sign that even Latin ecclesiastics are
furtively beginning to apply it.

Baur had approached theology through the
philosophy of Schleiermacher and Hegel. *"Ohne
Philosophie,"* he wrote, *"bleibt mir die Geschichte
ewig tod und stumm."*[1]   To Strauss also (born
1808, died 1874) philosophy was a first love,
and he too dreamed of framing Church history
in a niche of Hegel's system of logic.   He studied
at Blaubeuren under Baur, at Maulbronn, and
in Berlin, and in 1832 became a teacher in the
University of Tübingen, where he found his old

---

[1] "Without philosophy history remains for me ever
dead and dumb."

master Baur. His instinct was to devote himself to philosophical teaching, but the authorities
obliged him to remain attached to the theological
faculty, and the result was his *Leben Jesu,* or
"Life of Jesus," which appeared in 1835. The
work was a gigantic success. He woke up to
find himself famous, but an outcast without a
future. The conservatives denounced him to
the educational authorities, and he was deprived
of his modest appointment in the university.
Barely two or three of his friends had the courage
to take up the cudgels in his defence. His work
went through many editions, by no means re-
prints of one another. The third, for example,
made some concessions to the orthodox standpoint, which he took back in the later editions.
In 1839 the chair of *Dogmatic* at Zürich was
offered him, but there such an uproar was raised
by pietists that the Swiss authorities revoked
the appointment, giving him a small pension
instead. After that he spent a wandering and
rather unhappy life, turning his pen to profane
history and literary criticism, and writing among
other things a valuable monograph on Reimarus.
In 1864 he returned to theology, and published
A Life of Jesus for the German People.

In his preface to this he remarks on the happy
change which had taken place in public opinion
since 1835, when his enemies complained that
he might at least have concealed his thoughts

from the general public by writing in Latin. In fact, the very outcry against him, for being pitched in so shrill a key, had reached the ears of the multitude, and so drawn the attention of thousands to a subject of which they would otherwise have remained in ignorance. He closes this preface with an acknowledgment of the value of Renan's work, which had appeared in the interim. "A book," he writes, "which, almost before it appeared, was condemned by I know not how many bishops, and by the Roman Curia itself, must necessarily be a most useful book."

Strauss made a somewhat ungenerous attack on the French nation in 1870, which made him popular for a time among his countrymen, but which cannot be otherwise regarded than as a stain on a singularly noble and upright character. Beside his prose works, he wrote many elegant and touching poems.

Because Strauss summarily eliminated the supernatural element, it has been assumed that he turned the entire story of Jesus into myth— this by those who never read the book they denounced, and will hear nothing of a Christ who is not through and through a supernatural being.

The truth is that Strauss understood far better than the reactionaries of 1835 the conditions under which the gospels took shape, and the influences which moulded their narratives. His

DAVID F. STRAUSS.

critics argued that, since the first and fourth evangelists were eye-witnesses and took part in the miraculous episodes, their narratives cannot be myths in any sense whatever. Strauss replied that the outside evidence in favour of their having been eye-witnesses is slender, and the internal evidence *nil*. In this matter the subsequent development of opinion, even in orthodox Church circles, has endorsed Strauss's position. No one now contends that Matthew's Gospel is other than the work of an unknown writer who compiled it out of Mark's Gospel and Q, the common document of Matthew and Luke. As to John, Professor Sanday, the last upholder of it, sacrifices its historicity when he argues that none but an apostle would have taken such liberties with the life of his Master; and the Rev. J. M. Thompson,[1] who assuredly voices the opinion of the younger and better educated of the English clergy, pronounces this gospel to be "not a biography, but a treatise in theology." "Its author," he goes on to observe, "would be almost as ready to sacrifice historical truth where it clashes with his dogmatic purpose as he is (apparently) anxious to observe it where it illustrates his point."

Strauss displayed more insight than Baur when he declared that the single generation which elapsed between the death of Jesus and

[1] *Jesus According to St. Mark*, London, 1909, p. 11.

the date of the earliest gospel was amply long enough time for such mythical accretions as we find to gather about the memory of Jesus. Messianic ideas of the Old Testament, early aspirations of believers, the desire to conform the sparse records of his ministry to supposed prophecies and to parallel his figure with those of Moses and Elijah—these and many other influences rapidly generated in a credulous age and society the Saga-like tales of the gospels about his miraculous powers. These tales Strauss discussed in a chapter entitled "Storm, Sea, and Fish Stories."

Strauss was the first German writer to discern the emptiness for historical purposes of the Fourth Gospel, which Schleiermacher had invested with a halo of authority, and by which even Renan was deceived. He pronounced it to be a work of apologetic Christology, composed by a Gnostic who wished to uphold the flesh-and-blood reality of Jesus against other Gnostics who denied that reality and resolved him into a merely phantasmal being. Advanced critics in that age lauded this gospel because it contains so little eschatology. That single fact, replied Strauss, convicts it of being both late and false.

> Jesus [he wrote] in any case expected that he would set up the throne of David afresh, and with the help of his twelve disciples reign over a liberated people. Yet he never

set any trust in the swords of human followers (Luke xxii., 38, Matt. xxvi., 52), but only in the legions of angels, which his heavenly Father would send to his aid (Matt. xxvi., 53). Wherever he speaks of his advent in Messianic glory, it is with angels and heavenly Hosts (*i.e.*, not with human warriors) that he surrounds himself (Matt. xvi., 27, xxiv., 30 *ff.*, xxv., 31); before the majesty of a Son of Man coming in the clouds of heaven the Gentiles will bow without any drawing of swords, and at the call of the Angel's trumpet will along with the dead risen from their tombs submit themselves for judgment to him and his Twelve. But this consummation Jesus did not hope to effect by his own will; he left it to the heavenly Father, who alone knows the right moment at which to bring about the catastrophe (Mark xiii., 32), to give him the signal. That, he hoped, would save him from any error in supposing that the end was reached before due warning was given. Let those who would banish this point of view from the background of Jesus' Messianic plan and outlook, merely because it seems to turn him into a visionary, only reflect how exactly these hopes agreed with the long-cherished Messianic ideas of the Jews, and how easily even a sensible man, breathing the contemporary atmosphere of supernaturalism, and shut up in the narrow circle of Jewish nationality, might be drawn over to a belief, however superstitious in itself, provided only it embodied the national point of view and also contained certain elements of truth and grandeur.

The eschatological aspects of Jesus' Gospel could not be better summed up than in the above; and equally admirable are the remarks which follow on the Last Supper:

> When Jesus ended this feast with the words, *Henceforth I will not again drink of the 'fruit of the vine, until I drink it with you new in my Father's Kingdom*, he must have anticipated that the Passover would be celebrated in the Messianic kingdom with special solemnity. If, therefore, he assures his disciples that he will next enjoy this annually recurring feast, not in this, but in the next age (*æon*), that shows that he expected this pre-Messianic world-order to be removed and the Messianic to take its place within the year.

Here Strauss anticipates Wellhausen and other intelligent commentators of to-day. With the same firm insight he traces the gradual emergence in Jesus of the consciousness that he was himself the promised Messiah. In Matt. xii., 8, he remarks, here again anticipating the best recent criticism, that the *Son of Man* in the text, "*The Son of Man is Lord also of the Sabbath*," may mean simply *Man in general;* but in another class of passages, where Jesus speaks of the *Son of Man*, a supernatural person is intended wholly distinct from himself, as the Messiah generically. This, for example, is the natural interpretation of the passage Matt. x., 23, where at the sending forth of the disciples he assures them that they will not have completed their tour of the Jewish cities before the Son of Man shall come.   Here surely Jesus speaks of the Messiah as being himself the Messiah's forerunner.   In that case this utterance must belong to the earliest period of his career, before he recognised himself to be the Messiah.   As Dr. Schweitzer, to whom I am indebted for the above remarks, says (p. 89), Strauss hardly realised the importance of the remark which he here throws out, but it contains the kernel of the solution of the problem of the Son of Man recently provided by the most acute of German critics, Johannes Weiss.[1]

Strauss also goes far to explain the genesis of Paul's conception of Jesus as a pre-existent being. Jesus, he argues, clearly conceived of his Messianic *rôle* as involving this much—namely, that he, the Born of Earth, was to be taken up into heaven after he had completed his earthly career, and was to return thence in glory in order to inaugurate the Kingdom of God on earth.

Now, in the higher Jewish theology, immediately after the age of Jesus, we meet with the idea of a pre-existence of the Messiah. The supposition, therefore, lies near at hand that the same idea was already current at the

[1] *Die Predigt Jesu vom Reiche Gottes—i.e.,* "Jesus' Preaching of the Kingdom of God."   First edition 1892, second 1900.

time when Jesus was becoming known; and that—once he apprehended himself as Messiah—he may have appropriated to himself this further trait of Messianic portraiture. The only question is whether Jesus was so deeply initiated as Paul in the school-wisdom of his age, so as to have borrowed from it this notion.

That Jesus expected to come amid clouds and with the angelic hosts to usher in his kingdom is, according to Strauss, quite certain. The only question is whether he expected his own death to intervene, or only thought that the glorious moment would surprise him in the midst of this life. From Matt. x., 23 and xvi., 28 one might infer the latter. But it always remains possible that, supposing he later on came to anticipate his death as certain, his ideas may have shaped themselves by way of a final form into what is expressed in Matt. xxvi., 64.

Strauss's chief defect was that he did not pay enough attention to the relations in which the Synoptic gospels stand to one another, and his neglect of this problem obscured for him many features of the first and third gospels. Like Schleiermacher, he believed Mark's gospel to be a mere compilation from the other two, and regarded it as a satellite of Matthew's gospel without any light of its own. The many graphic touches which distinguish this gospel were, so he argued, Saga-like exaggerations of the compiler. His work would have gained in clearness and grasp if he had understood that Mark's gospel forms the basis of the other two Synoptists, and furnishes them with the order in which they arrange their incidents. Without this clue a critic or commentator is sure to go beating about the bush after the manner of an old-fashioned harmonist, here laying stress on Matthew's sequence of events, there upon Luke's; whereas, in point of fact, neither of them had any real guide except Mark, from whose order of events they only departed in order to pursue that of their unassisted imaginations.

The circumstances of Renan's life are so well known that I need not repeat them. Who has not read that most exquisite of autobiographies, the *Souvenirs d' Enfance et de Jeunesse*, in which he leads us along the path of his intellectual emancipation from being the inmate of a clerical seminary, first in his native Breton village and then in Paris, to becoming the author of *The Life of Jesus, The Apostles* (1866),[1] *St. Paul* (1869), *Antichrist* (1873), *The Gospels* (1877), *Marcus Aurelius* (1881). These volumes will continue to be read for their glamour of style, no less than for their candour and nobility of sentiment; for on all that he wrote, however technical and learned the subject-matter, Renan

[1] Translated by W. G. Hutchison for the R. P. A., 1905.

ERNEST RENAN.

145

set the stamp of his character and personality. But these volumes also impress us by the vast learning which lies behind them. German theologians too often overwhelm us by their learning, and in reading them we cannot see the wood for the trees. But Renan never committed this fault. Hardly a page of his that does not help us to a clear perspective of the period and subject he is handling. He contrasts with clumsy but learned writers like Keim, as a grace‧ ful, symmetrical city like Perugia set on a hill amid Italian skies contrasts with an English manufacturing city, a planless congeries of vulgar abominations framed in grime and smoke and dirt. The fanatics chased Renan in 1862 from the chair he held of Semitic Studies, and he was only restored by the French Republic in 1871; but he was not in the least embittered by the experience, and, in spite of their volleys of execration, he continued to the end to cherish the kindliest feelings towards a clergy he had so narrowly escaped from joining.

Of the works enumerated *The Life of Jesus*, though it is the best known, is not the most valuable; for when he wrote it Renan was still under the spell of the fourth gospel, and inclined to use it as an embodiment of genuine traditions unknown to and therefore unrecorded by the three other evangelists. Then, again, his portraiture of Jesus as a simpering, sentimental person, sometimes stooping to tricks, must grate upon many who yet are not in the least devout believers.

There is thus some justification for Schweitzer's verdict that it is waxworks, lyrical and stagey. Renan, however, in approaching the study of the gospels, had at least the great advantage of being a good Hebrew and Talmudic scholar; and only want of space forbids me to cite many excellent passages inspired by this lore. The single one I can give is from *Les Évangiles*, p. 97, and bears on the date of the Synoptic Gospels:

> We doubt whether this collection of narratives, aphorisms, parables, prophetic citations, can have been committed to writing earlier than the death of the Apostles and before the destruction of Jerusalem. It is towards the year 75 that we conjecturally set the moment at which were sketched out the features of that image before which eighteen centuries have knelt. Batanéa, where the brethren of Jesus lived, and whither the remains of the Church of Jerusalem had fled, seems to have been the district where this important work was accomplished. The language used was that in which Jesus' own words—words that men knew by heart— were couched; that is to say, the Syro-Chaldaic, wrongly denominated Hebrew. Jesus' brethren and the refugee Christians from Jerusalem spoke this language, which indeed

differed little from that of such inhabitants of Batanéa as had not adopted Greek. It was in this dialect, obscure and devoid of literary culture, that was traced the first pencil sketch of the book which has charmed so many souls. No doubt, if the Gospel had remained a Hebrew or Syriac book, its fortunes would soon have been cut short. It was in a Greek dress that the Gospel was destined to reach perfection and assume the final form in which it has gone round the world. Still we must not forget that the Gospel was, to begin with, a Syrian book, written in a Semitic language. The style of the Gospel, that charming trick of childlike narrative which recalls the limpidest pages of the old Hebrew Scriptures, pervaded by a sort of ideal ether that the ancient people knew not, has in it nothing Hellenic. It is based on Hebrew.

In this volume Renan corrected the error into which he had fallen of overrating the historical value of the fourth gospel. His appreciations of the other gospels are very just, and he rightly rejects the opinion, which still governed most minds, that the second gospel is a compilation from the first and third.

CHAPTER VIII

ENGLISH WORK

FAR back in the nineteenth century the task of introducing to the English public in translations the works of the more scholarly and open - minded German theologians was already begun, and Strauss's *Life of Jesus* was twice published in our tongue, first in 1846, and again in 1865. The earlier translator deplores the fact that "no *respectable* English publisher" would attempt the publication of his book "from a fear of persecution." The Anglican clergy, much more the Nonconformist, remained untouched by the new learning until the last two or three decades of that century; and it is a significant fact that the only work of its middle time which really threw light on the composition of the gospels, or would have done so could any one in theological circles have been induced to read it, was the work of a layman, James Smith, of Jordanhill, a leading geologist and a F.R.S. In his *Dissertation on the Origin and Connection of the Gospels* (Black-

149

wood, 1853) we find an abundance of shrewd surmises and conclusions. Thus, *à propos* of the multiplicity of readings found in MSS.—a multiplicity which sorely scandalised the believers in verbal inspiration, who were puzzled to say which one of ten different readings in a single passage was due to the Holy Ghost rather than to a copyist—Smith remarks that "there is a greater amount of verbal agreement in the more modern MSS. than we find in the earliest existing ones." Here is a truth to which critics are only just now waking up—viz., that the text was never in any degree fixed until it was canonised and consecrated. Till then it was more or less in flux. For the rest, Smith argued that Luke and Matthew used the Hebrew original, of which Mark was the translator, rather than that they used our Mark. This was an error, but an error in the direction of the truth. It is impossible, however, to acquiesce in the view that the agreement between Matthew and Mark is translational only, except in so far as Mark in rendering his source (as to which Smith accepted Papias's tradition that he was interpreter of Peter) made much use of an earlier version of the same made by Matthew. Luke, he believed, wrote with both Mark and Matthew before him.

But Smith's real achievement was to overthrow the old superstition that inspired evan-

gelists could not have written at all except
in complete independence of one another, and
without the servile necessity of copying common documents. English divines rightly felt
that the citadel of inspiration was breached if
it were once proved that the Evangelists copied
either one another or common documents; and
sound criticism could not take root among
them until this prejudice was dispelled. It
has practically vanished to-day; but it vanished
tardily, and divines are now employed in de-
vising plasters and bandages to cover the
wounds inflicted on their faith. It seems
strange that nineteenth-century divines could
not admit what, as James Smith remarks,
was obvious to the early Fathers; yet so it was.
For example, Augustine wrote thus of the
Evangelists:—

> We do not find that they were minded,
> each of them, to write as if he was ignorant
> of his fellow who went before him, nor that
> the one left out by ignorance what we find
> another writing.[1]

Augustine also believed that Mark had Matthew before him, and followed him.

Even the celebrated Dr. Lardner, in his
History of the Apostles and Evangelists, was
wedded to this hypothesis of the mutual inde-

---

[1] *De Cons. Evang.*, i., c. i.

pendence of the gospels. He and others of his age deemed it to be evident from the nature and design of the first three gospels that their authors had not seen any authentic history of Jesus Christ; and the fact that the Synoptists "have several things peculiar to themselves" was held to "show that they did not borrow from each other[1];" yet more "the seeming [mark well the meiosis of the professional divine!] contradictions which exist in the first three gospels" were adduced as "evidence that the Evangelists did not write by concert, or after having seen each other's gospels."

Dr. Davidson, a comparatively liberal divine, and one who suffered for his liberality, argued in the same way in his *Introduction to the New Testament.* Smith, however, wrote in answer as follows:

> There is not a single phenomenon adduced in proof that the Evangelists made no use of the works of their predecessors, but what may be met with in these modern contemporary historians, in cases where we know that they did make use of the works of their predecessors.

This position he proved incontestably by confronting in parallel columns narratives of the same incidents written by Sir Archibald Alison

[1] So Horne in his now forgotten *Introduction to the Bible.*

in his *History of the French Revolution*, by General Napier, and by Suchet in his *Memoirs* of the war in Spain. Napier was an eye-witness, and also used Suchet. Alison used both. To the divines of that generation who fell back on the soft option of oral tradition, because that alternative was to their minds least incompatible with verbal inspiration, Smith replied in words which put the matter in a nutshell. He writes (p. xlviii.):

> A stereotyped cyclus of oral tradition never did nor ever can exist. Even poetry cannot be repeated without variations.
>
> There is one phenomenon peculiar to compositions derived from the same written sources, which may be termed the phenomenon of tallying. The writers may add matter drawn from other sources, or they leave out passages; but ever and anon they return to the original authority, where they will be found to tally with each other; but it is only in such cases that such correspondences occur. Hence, when they do occur, we are warranted in inferring the existence of a written original.

Mr. W. G. Rushbrooke, at the instance and with the assistance of the Rev. Dr. Edwin A. Abbott,[1] Headmaster of the City of London

---

[1] With the collaboration of another distinguished Cambridge scholar, Dr. Hort.

School, finally settled the matter ,in a work entitled *Synopticon* (London, 1880). In this he arranged in parallel columns the texts of Mark, Matthew, and Luke, picking out in red whatever is common to all three, and in other distinctive types whatever any two of them share in common. The originality of Mark was thus demonstrated once for all. There are barely half-a-dozen passages which suggest that Matthew had access to the ulterior documents used by Mark; so complete is his dependence on the latter, as he has been transmitted to us. It was not, of course, a new view. Herder had discerned the fact, and the German scholar Lachmann had pointed out as early as 1835, in his *Studien und Kritiken*, that Mark provided the mould in which the matter of Matthew and Luke was cast. "The diversity of order in the gospel narratives is," he wrote, "not so great as appears to many. It is greatest if you compare them all with one another, or Luke with Matthew; small if you compare Mark separately with the other two." In other words, Mark provides the common term between Luke and Matthew. The matter is so plain if we glance at a single page of the *Synopticon* that one wonders at any one ever having had any doubts about it.

And here we are led to refer to the famous controversy between Bishop Lightfoot and the author of a work entitled *Supernatural Religion*, of which the first edition appeared in 1874 anonymously from the pen of Mr. Walter R. Cassels. In that work it was argued that *our* Gospels of Matthew and Mark cannot be those signified by Papias, whose words, as quoted by Eusebius, run thus:

> Mark became the interpreter of Peter, and wrote down accurately as much as he (? Mark or Peter) remembered (*or* reminded him of), not, however, in order, of what was either said or done by Christ. For he neither heard the Lord, nor was one of his followers; but later on became, as I have said, a follower of Peter, who suited his teachings to people's needs, without making an orderly array of the Dominical words; so that Mark committed no error in thus writing down certain things as he could recollect them; for his one concern was to omit nothing he heard, and to falsify nothing therein.
>
> Matthew, however, composed (*or* set in order) the Logia (*or* oracles) in the Hebrew dialect, and every one interpreted them as best he could.

Lightfoot waxed ironical, because the author of *Supernatural Religion* questioned if our Mark were the same as the Mark of Papias. But, if Papias's Matthew was quite another document than ours, why not also his Mark?—the more so

because his description of Mark as a work devoid of chronological order ill suits the Mark
which stands in our Bibles; for the latter is
most careful about the order of events, and provides a skeleton order for the other two Evangelists.   Except in so far as they both follow
Mark, the two other Synoptists exhibit no
order of events whatever.

For the rest, Lightfoot proved that his antagonist misinterpreted Eusebius's use of Papias.   For where the historian merely states
that Papias used and quoted certain books of
the New Testament—like the Johannine Epistles—which, as not being accepted by all the
Churches, were called *Antilegomena*, Mr. Cassels over-hastily inferred Eusebius to mean that
Papias did not know of other cognate Scriptures universally received in the Eusebian age;
for example, the fourth gospel.   In the case
of generally received books, Eusebius was not
concerned to inform us whether or not he had
found them cited in Papias, and therefore in
such cases no argument can be based on his
silence.   Papias may or may not have had
them.   We only know for certain that he had
those of the *Antilegomena*, which Eusebius
declares he had.

The Bishop was also able to pick a few holes
in his adversary's scholarship, and to refute his
thesis that our Luke is merely a later edition of

Marcion's Gospel. He could not, however, touch the chapter on the Authorship and Character of the Fourth Gospel, and had nothing to oppose to the remarkable opening chapters on Miracles, except the usual commonplaces of hazy pietism. In critical outlook Lightfoot held no superiority, though he was a better scholar and, within the narrow circle of his premises, a more careful and accurate worker.

Not that, on the other hand, the book he criticised has not grave shortcomings. In general it underestimates the external evidence in favour of the age of the Synoptic gospels; and its author has no clear idea either of the relations in which they stand to each other, or of the supreme importance of ascertaining those relations correctly. He moved exclusively in the circle of Baur's ideas, and had neglected other German books of equal weight, like those of C. H. Weisse and C. G. Wilke, published in 1838. The index of the book has no reference to the eschatology of the gospels and of Paul; and to this important subject it contains few, and those few the most meagre, references. In all these respects, however, Dr. Lightfoot was as poorly equipped as Mr. Cassels.

Another famous controversy which aroused the Oxford and Cambridge of my youth (1880–1890) was that of Dean Burgon with the Re-

visers of the English Bible, and especially
of the New Testament. This quarrel raged
around the so-called Received Text, or *Textus
Receptus*. Before the year 1633 such a term
was unknown; but in that year the Elzevir firm
in Leiden and Amsterdam issued a slightly
revised text of Beza's New Testament (of 1565),
which was, in turn, little more than a reprint
of Stephanus's or Estienne's fourth edition of
1551. That, in turn, was a reprint of a large
edition called the *Regia*, or Royal, which gave
Erasmus's first text with variants from fifteen
MSS., and from the Spanish Editio Princeps
of Alcala. Erasmus's edition was based on
half-a-dozen late MSS. Now, an unknown
scholar who prepared this edition of 1633 wrote
in his preface the words: "Here, then, you
have the text now received by all, in which we
give nothing altered or corrupt."

Altered from what? There was no standard, save the earlier editions, and these represented only a score or so of the 1300 cursive
MSS. now known to exist, and not a single one
of the twelve great uncial MSS. of the gospels
ranging from the fourth to the ninth century.
During the eighteenth century further editions
were issued of the New Testament by such
scholars as John Mill, Wells, Bentley, and Mace
in England; by Bengel, Wettstein, Semler,
Griesbach, and Matthäi abroad, who continually

W. J. Burgon
Dean of Chichester.

159

collated fresh MSS. and ancient versions, either
adding the new variants below the text or even
introducing them into the text. In the nineteenth century Carl Lachmann (1831) issued at
Berlin the first really scientific text of the New
Testament. He followed the earliest MSS., and
gave weight to the very ancient Latin versions
of Africa and Italy. He remarked that an
editor who confined himself to the most ancient
sources could find no use for the so-called Received Text; and he accordingly relegated the
readings of this to the obscurity of an appendix.
He followed up this edition with later ones in
1842 and 1850, expanding each time his critical
apparatus.[1]

If Lachmann had been an orthodox divine, he
might have shrunk from such innovations; but
he was primarily a classical scholar, concerned
with the texts of Homer, Lucretius, and other
profane authors; and he merely brought to the
study of the New Testament text the critical
canons and the principles of candour and hon-
esty in common vogue among classical philolo-
gists. But he reaped the reward of unpopularity
which is in store for all who discover anything
that is new or true in the field of religion. The

[1] *Critical apparatus* is the technical term for the tabu-
lated textual variants taken from MSS. and added, sometimes with conjectural emendations of the editor himself,
underneath a classical text.

pietists had been growling for over a century
at the number of various readings printed by
scholars in their editions of the New Testament,
and cudgelling their brains how to reconcile all
these diversities of text and meaning with the
supposed inspiration of the book. To such
minds Lachmann's edition, which set aside
with contempt the entire *Textus Receptus*,
savoured of open blasphemy, and in a hundred
keys they let him know it. But the world was
moving, and the new developments of Old
Testament criticism encouraged students of the
New Testament to bolder flights. Colenso
seemed to suffer for the advancement of Hebrew
studies only; but the persecutions he endured
nerved younger men with honest hearts to undertake the study of the New Testament in the
same free spirit. In Germany Constantine
Tischendorf carried on the good work of Lachmann, discovering and editing many new MSS.,
and in particular the great uncial of the Con-
vent of Sinai, called by scholars *Aleph*. In
England Scrivener, Tregelles, Westcott, and
Hort devoted their lives to the accumulation of
new material and to the preparation of better
editions.

At last, in 1870, the English clergy awoke to
the fact that the Received Text as given in the
old authorised version of King James's translators was no longer satisfactory, and the two

11

Houses of Convocation appointed a body of revisers to prepare a new English version. This was issued in 1881, and the editors state in their preface the reasons which justified its appearance. The editions of Stephanus and Beza, and the Complutensian Polyglott, from which the authorised English version was made, were, they allege, "based on manuscripts of late date, few in number, and used with little critical skill."

This Revised Version of 1881 marks a great advance in interpretation in so far as it is based on the earliest known MSS., and especially on the great uncials; and also in that, wherever practicable, it adheres to the same English equivalent of a Greek word or phrase. This uniformity in the rendering of the same words enables a student who knows no Greek to trace out accurately the triple and double traditions in the texts of the gospels. Its defects briefly are, firstly, that, owing to the number of the scholars employed in revising, and the difficulty of getting them to agree, the text often has the patchwork appearance of a compromise; and, secondly, that, inasmuch as they were orthodox and somewhat timid divines, the more orthodox of two or more ancient readings or interpretations is commonly printed in the text, the rival ones being consigned to the margin or altogether

ignored for fear of shocking the weaker brethren.
A genuine scholar detects on many a page of it
the work of rather weak-kneed people.

None the less it was too strong meat for the
run of the English clergy, who found a spokes-
man in the Rev. William Burgon, a Fellow of
Oriel College in Oxford, vicar of the University
Church, and finally Dean of Chichester, an old-
fashioned scholar of much learning, and a master
of mordant wit and incisive language. He
fell upon his fellow-divines with a fury which
provoked much amusement among the scoffers,
and if his bon-mots could have been printed
in a cheap form and disseminated among the
crowd, I venture to think they would have
been more effective than all the lectures of
Mr. Bradlaugh and Colonel Ingersoll for the
cause that those lecturers had at heart. I
copy out a few *flosculi* from the good Dean's
articles in the *Quarterly Review*, entitled "The
Revision Revised," and from his Epistle of
Protest addressed to Bishop Ellicott, who
had acted as president of the committee of
Revisers.

Drs. Westcott and Hort, of Cambridge,
were by far the most competent of the Revisers, who as a rule deferred, and wisely, to
their judgment, taking as their standard the
Greek text of the New Testament prepared by

them. Of these scholars, therefore, Burgon writes:

> The absolute absurdity (I use the word advisedly) of Westcott and Hort's New Textual Theory. . . .
>
> In their solemn pages an attentive reader finds himself encountered by nothing but a series of unsupported assumptions. . . .
>
> Their (so-called) "Theory" is in reality nothing else but a weak effort of the imagination.

Of the Revision itself he writes:

> It is the most astonishing as well as the most calamitous literary blunder of the age. . . .
>
> Their [the Revisers'] uncouth phraseology and their jerky sentences, their pedantic obscurity and their unidiomatic English. . . .
>
> The systematic depravation of the underlying Greek is nothing else but a poisoning of the River of Life at its sacred source. Our Revisers (with the best and purest intentions, no doubt) stand convicted of having deliberately rejected the words of inspiration in every page. . . .

Of the five oldest Greek manuscripts on which the Revisers relied, called by scholars for sake of reference *Aleph* A B C D, the Dean writes that they

> are among the most corrupt documents extant. Each of these codices (*Aleph* B D) clearly exhibits a fabricated text—is the result of arbitrary and reckless recension. . . .

The two most weighty of these codices, *Aleph* and B, he likens to the "two false witnesses" of Matt. xxvi., 60. Of these two I have supplied my readers with facsimiles (see pp. 9 and 48).

But it is on Bishop Ellicott that he empties out the vials of his wrath in such terms as the following:

> You, my Lord Bishop, who have never gone deeply into the subject, repose simply on *prejudice*. Never having at any time collated codices *Aleph* A B C D for yourself, you are unable to gainsay a single statement of mine by a counter-appeal to *facts*. Your textual learning proves to have been all obtained at second-hand. . . .
>
> Did you ever take the trouble to collate a sacred MS.? If you ever did, pray with *what* did you make your collation? . . .
>
> You flout me: you scold me: you lecture me. But I do not find that you ever *answer* me. You reproduce the theory of Drs. Westcott and Hort—which I claim to have demolished. . . . Denunciation, my Lord Bishop, is not argument; neither is reiteration proof. . . .
>
> Not only have you, on countless occasions, thrust out words, clauses, entire sentences, of genuine Scripture, but you have been careful that no trace shall survive of the fatal injury which you have inflicted. I wonder you were not afraid. Can I be wrong in deeming such a proceed-

ing in a high degree sinful? Has not the
SPIRIT pronounced a tremendous doom
against those who do such things (Rev.
xxii., 19)?

The Revisers had admitted among their
number a learned Unitarian minister, Dr. G.
Vance Smith. This, writes Burgon, is, "it
seems to me, nothing else but an insult to our
Divine Master and a wrong to the Church."
Of the marginal note set by the Revisers against
Romans ix., 5, he complains that it is "a Socinian
gloss gratuitously thrust into the margin of
every Englishman's New Testament."
Poor Dean Farrar escapes with an expression
of contempt for his "hysterical remarks."
Nevertheless, in his saner moments Burgon
entertained a very just ideal of textual criticism, and in the same volume from which I have
made the above quotations he writes (p. 125)
as follows:

> The *fundamental principles* of the science
> of textual criticism are not yet apprehended.
> . . . Let a generation of students give
> themselves entirely up to this neglected
> branch of sacred science. Let 500 more
> copies of the Gospels, Acts, and Epistles be
> diligently collated. Let at least 100 of the
> ancient *Lectionaries* be very exactly collated
> also. Let the most important versions be
> edited afresh, and let the languages in

which these are written be for the first
time really *mastered* by Englishmen. *Above
all, let the Fathers be called upon to give up
their precious secrets.* Let their writings be
ransacked and indexed, and (where needful)
let the MSS. of their works be diligently
inspected, in order that we may know what
actually *is* the evidence which they afford.
Only so will it ever be possible to obtain a
Greek text on which absolute reliance may
be placed, and which may serve as the basis
for a satisfactory revision of our Authorised
Version.

It is a curious indication of the muddle into
which theological *arrière pensée* can get otherwise honest men that almost in the same breath
Burgon could prejudge the question at issue
and write as follows (Feb. 21, 1887) to Lord
Cranbrook:

> You will understand then that, in brief,
> my object is to vindicate the Traditional
> Text of the New Testament against all its
> past and present assailants, and to establish
> it on such a basis of security *that it may be
> incapable of being effectually disturbed any
> more.* I propose myself to lay down logi-
> cal principles, and to *demonstrate* that men
> have been going wrong for the last fifty
> years, and to explain how this has come to
> pass in every instance, and to get them to
> admit their error. At least, I will con-
> vince every fair person that the truth is

what I say it is—viz., that in nine cases out of ten the *commonly received text* is the true one.

There was some ground then for the gibe that Burgon's one aim was to canonise the misprints of a sixteenth-century printer. He was, in fact, upholding a paradox; he would not—perhaps could not, so dense was the veil of prejudice with which the old theory of inspiration covered his eyes—see that prior to the collection of the gospels in a canon, about the year 180, and while they were still circulating singly in isolated churches, their text was less fixed and more liable to changes, doctrinal and transcriptional, than they ever were afterwards; and that the ultimate text, if there ever was one that deserves to be so called, is for ever irrecoverable. The *reductio ad absurdum* of his bias for the Received, or rather Vulgar, text was, as might be expected, provided by himself. The passage is so picturesque as to merit to be cited in its integrity:

I request that the clock of history may be put back 1700 years. This is A.D. 183, if you please; and—indulge me in the supposition!—you and I are walking in Alexandria. We have reached the house of one Clemens, a learned Athenian who has long been a resident here. Let us step into his library—he is from home. What a queer place! See, he has been reading his

Bible, which is open at St. Mark x. Is it not a well-used copy? It must be at least fifty or sixty years old. Well, but suppose only thirty or forty. It was executed, therefore, *within fifty years of the death of St. John the Evangelist.* Come, let us transcribe two of the columns (σελίδες) as faithfully as we possibly can, and be off. . . . We are back in England again, and the clock has been put right. Now let us sit down and examine our curiosity at leisure. . . . It proves on inspection to be a transcript of the fifteen verses (ver. 17 to ver. 31) which relate to the coming of the rich young ruler to our Lord.

We make a surprising discovery. . . . It is impossible to produce a 'fouler exhibition of St. Mark x., 17–31 than is contained in a document older than either B. or Aleph—itself the property of one of the most 'famous of the ante-Nicene Fathers. . . . The foulness of a text which must have been penned within seventy or eighty years of the death of the last of the Evangelists is a matter of fact, which must be loyally accepted and made the best of.

The Revised Version, as any one will have noticed who has compared it with the old authorised texts, omits an enormous number of passages, some of which were of great beauty and pathos. Accordingly Dean Goulburn, Burgon's friend, partisan, and biographer, writes (*Life of J. W. Burgon*, ii., 213) thus:—

Are not these three passages alone—the

record of the agony, the record of the first
saying on the cross, and the doxology of the
Lord's Prayer—passages of such value as to
make it wrong and cruel to shake the faith
of ordinary Bible readers in them?

Here is a pragmatist argument indeed. Truth
is to be sacrificed to efficiency in practical
working. In the same temper Canon Liddon
had written to Burgon lamenting that the Revision had been conducted more as if it were a
literary enterprise than a religious one. Neither
Burgon nor his friends seem to have had any
idea that, by issuing a translation that is not as
exact a representation as possible of the oldest
and most authentic texts procurable, you com-
mit in the field of religion the same sort of
crime as a forger does in the commercial world
by uttering base coin or flash bank-notes. No
Jesuits were ever more tortuous in their methods.
In his *Introduction to the First Three Gospels*
(Berlin, 1905, p. 6), J. Wellhausen sums up
Burgon's position by saying that the further the
manuscript tradition stretches back, the worse
it becomes. Grey hairs, he laconically adds,
cannot always save a divine from making a
fool of himself.[1] Even admirers of Burgon
had their misgivings roused by such outbursts

[1] "Richtig ist allerdings, dass Alter nicht vor Thorheit
schützt."

as the one I have cited.   If water choked them, what had they left to drink?   If the two most ancient of our uncial codices, Vaticanus B and the Sinaitic Aleph, are false witnesses against Christ, and if our oldest ascertainable texts of the second century excel in "foulness," then what corruptions may not lurk in later texts, time and the mechanical errors of scribes being the sole factors in change which the orthodox would allow?   There is no doubt that such verdicts from one so indisputably orthodox and learned as the Dean of Chichester helped to unsettle the minds of the clergy and educated laymen and that they prepared the way for the outspoken criticisms of the *Encyclopedia Biblica*.

A tendency has long been visible in the Anglican Communion to lighten the ship by jettisoning the books of Moses; and the most recent results (we write in 1910) of New Testament textual criticism have still further undermined faith.   The old bulldog-like confidence of Burgon and Liddon is seldom shown to-day. Mr. Robert Anderson, one of the few whose robust orthodoxy is still proof against any and all reasoning in these domains, justly states the position of the *Lux Mundi* school as follows:

The Bible is not infallible, but the Church is infallible, and upon the authority of the Church our faith can find a sure foundation. But how do we know that the Church is to be trusted? The ready answer is, We know it upon the authority of the Bible. That is to say, we trust the Bible on the authority of the Church, and we trust the Church on the authority of the Bible. It is a bad case of "the confidence trick" (*The Silence of God*, 1898, p. 92).

It remains to be seen whether in the century on the threshold of which we stand the authority of the thaumaturgic priest will survive that of the Bible; and whether the critics, having finally discredited the New Testament, will not turn their bulls'-eyes on to the history of the Church and Sacraments. In this task they will have a powerful ally in the new sciences of comparative religion and anthropology, just as they may have a relentless enemy in an electorate in which women may command a clear majority of votes. It has been said that Christianity began with women and will end with them. It is certainly the case that they are more easily imposed upon by priests than are men, more attracted by pomp of vestments, by music, lights, incense, auricular confession, and magic of sacraments, less prone to ask about any doctrine or ceremony presented to them under the rubric of faith and religion the questions: Is it true? On what evidence does it repose?

Has it any rational meaning, any historical basis?

This dissatisfaction with the Bible as a standard of faith is beginning also to be felt in the Latin Communion; and is really voiced by the distinguished Oxford Catholic, Father Joseph Rickaby, whom I have already had occasion to cite, in the following passage[1]:

> In the Gospels and Acts we do not possess one tenth of the evidence that carried conviction to Dionysius on the Areopagus, and to Apollos at Ephesus. We are still beset with the old Protestant Article, that everything worth a Christian's knowing was put down in black and white once and for all in the pages of the New Testament.

In the sequel he declares that "the glad tidings" which travelled "by word of mouth" from Peter and John and Paul to their disciples, and from these "through all generations"—that these "have not dried up into parchments; they are something over and above the *Codex Sinaiticus*." He admits that "the written narratives of the New Testament are difficult to harmonise, and leave strange gaps and lacunæ"; but he is not distressed by that, and, much as "he believes in the Word of the Gospel . . . still more does he believe in the word

[1] P. 143 of the volume *Jesus or Christ?* London, 1909.

of the Church." It is a pity that he does not specify in what particulars the Church's unwritten tradition supplements the gaps and lacunæ of the New Testament, or reconciles the many contradictions of its narratives. We seem to read between his lines this, that he is ready to let the critics have their way with the written records of his religion, if only the Church can be held together in some other way, her rites and sacraments guaranteed, and the sacerdotalist positions secured. It is probable that the Church can provide a canon of lead more pliable than the cast-iron rule of the letter. This ecclesiastic, we feel, is well on his way to become a modernist as far as the Scriptures are concerned.

CHAPTER IX

The Modernists

RECENT encyclicals of Pope Pius X. speak of the Modernists as if they formed a close sect; yet on closer inspection they are seen to be detached workers in various fields—in literature, like Fogazzaro; in philosophy and religion, like Father Tyrrell and Baron von Hugel; in Hebrew philosophy, like Minocchi; in Assyriology, Hebrew, and New Testament exegesis, like Alfred Loisy; in Church history, like Albert Houtin. All of them good Catholics, and only desirous of remaining members of their Church, they were only united in their desire to raise its scholarship and thinking to a modern critical level. Loisy was born 1857, and already as a young man made himself a name. He held the Chair of Assyriology and Hebrew in the Catholic Institute of Paris till 1892, when he was deprived, because he was too much of a scholar and a gentleman to stoop to the forced explanations and artificial combinations of a Vigouroux. He then took up the study of the

New Testament, but continued to lecture at the School of Higher Studies on Biblical Exegesis, drawing large audiences, largely composed of clerics. These lectures he ceased in March, 1904, at the instance of the Pope. In 1903 he followed up his little book, *The Gospel and the Church*, which had given much offence, with an ample commentary on the fourth gospel, in which he pulverised the old view of its apostolic authorship. The Papal Biblical Commissioners alluded to above were interrogated about it, and issued an absurd counterblast. Loisy's great commentary, in two volumes, on the Synoptic gospels followed in the spring of 1907, just before a Papal bull of major excommunication declared him to be a *homo vitandus qui ab omnibus vitari debet*—"a man to be avoided, whom every one is bound to avoid." A Latin Bishop in Great Britain publishing such a document would render himself liable to imprisonment for malicious libel. Except, however, that his charwoman gave him notice and left, Loisy sustained no harm, for the Pope's spiritual weapons are almost as antiquated as the old muskets I have seen in the hands of his Swiss guards. In the following year Loisy was chosen Professor of Ecclesiastical History in the University of Paris, in succession to the late-lamented Jean Réville, the author of exhaustive works on the early history of the Episcopate and on the fourth gospel. Not content with the magnificent advertisement of excommunication, the Pope supplied another, yet ampler, by issuing in July, 1907, an encyclical (beginning *Lamentabili sane exitu*) in which were condemned sixty-five theses drawn, or supposed by the Pope and his inquisitors to be drawn, from Loisy's works. Though in these theses Loisy's conclusions are often falsified or exaggerated, they are, on the whole, an apt summary of the most recent and assured results of criticism; and their dissemination must have damaged the cause of the Modernists about as much as a formal condemnation of Euclid's axioms would damage geometricians. The following are some of the propositions condemned:

15. The gospels, until the canon was defined and fixed, were amplified by continual additions and corrections. There survived in them, therefore, only tenuous and uncertain vestiges of Christ's teaching.

16. The narratives of John are not, properly speaking, history, but a mystical envisagement of the gospel. The discourses in it are theological meditations on the mystery of salvation devoid of historical truth.

21. The Revelation, which forms the object of Catholic faith, was not completed with the Apostles.

22. The dogmas which the Church regards as revealed are not truths fallen from heaven, but a sort of interpretation of religious facts at which the human mind arrived by laborious efforts.

27. The divinity of Jesus Christ cannot be proved from the gospels; it is a dogma deduced by the Christian conscience from the notion of the Messiah.

30. In all the gospel texts the name *Son of God* is equivalent only to the title *Messiah;* it in no way signified that Christ was the true and natural son of God.

31. The teaching about Christ handed down by Paul, John, and the Councils of Nice, Ephesus, and Chalcedon is not that which Jesus taught, but only what Christians had come to think about Jesus.

32. The natural sense of the gospel texts cannot be reconciled with what our theologians teach about the consciousness and infallible knowledge of Jesus Christ.

33. It is evident to any one not led away by his prejudices either that Jesus taught an error about the immediate advent of the Messiah, or that the greater part of his teaching as contained in the Synoptic gospels is unauthentic.

34. Criticism cannot attribute to Christ knowledge without bounds or limit, except on the hypothesis, inconceivable historically and

repugnant to modern feeling, that Christ as man possessed God's knowledge, and yet was unwilling to communicate a knowledge of so many things to his disciples and to posterity.

35. Christ was not from the first conscious of being the Messiah.

37. Faith in Christ's resurrection was, to begin with, less a belief in the fact itself than in his being immortal and alive in God's presence.

38. The doctrine of the expiatory death of Christ is not in the gospels, but was originated by Paul alone.

43. The custom of conferring baptism on infants was part of an evolution of discipline which eventually led to this sacrament being resolved into two—viz., Baptism and Penance.

45. In Paul's account of the institution of the Eucharist (1 Cor., xi. 23–25) we must not take everything historically.

49. As the Christian Supper little by little assumed the character of a liturgical action, so those who were accustomed to preside at it acquired a sacerdotal character.

51. Marriage could become a sacrament of the New Law only fairly late in the Church, etc.

52. It was foreign to the mind of Christ to set up a Church as a society which was to endure through long ages upon the earth. On the contrary, he imagined that the Kingdom of

Heaven and the end of the world were both equally imminent.

55. Simon Peter never dreamed of primacy in the Church having been conferred on him by Christ.

56. The promotion of the Roman Church to be head of other Churches was due to no arrangements of Divine Providence, but purely to political conditions.

60. Christian teaching was Jewish to begin with, though by successive evolutions it afterwards became, first Pauline, then Johannine, and finally Hellenic and universal.

65. Modern Catholicism can compound with genuine science only by transforming itself into a sort of undogmatic Christianity—that is, into a broad and liberal Protestantism.

Needless to say, these principles are largely exemplified in the lives and writings of our younger English clergy; and Professor Sanday, in his latest work on *Christologies*, declares that *we must modernise, whether we will or no.* He accordingly argues that the division in Jesus between the Divine and Human was not vertical, as the Fathers imagined, so that his waking actions and thoughts could be apportioned now to one, now to the other class. It was rather horizontal, his divine consciousness being only subliminal, and all the rest of him purely human. So I find that, as M. Jourdain

had all his life been talking prose without know-
ing it, I have been believing all along in an incarnation which Jesus at best shared with his
fellow-men. But to be quite serious: this view
hardly does justice to the mind and character of
Jesus, even in the eyes of those who deny that
he was in any way unique among men. For
the subliminal self is no better than a store-
house of past experiences and memories, some
of them possibly ante-natal, of the individual;
and it is chiefly revealed under abnormal and
diseased cerebral conditions. At best it is a
stepping-stone of the dead self on which "to
rise to higher things." Moral achievements and
character imply more, and are the work of a
creative will generating new results that never
pre-existed in any form; and we enter an *impasse*
if we try to explain conscious experiences and
efforts of will as the mere unwinding of a coiled
spring, as the unfolding of an eternal order
already implicit in things. For in the spiritual
domain the past does not wholly contain the
future; and no moral or speculative end is
served by trying to deduce our lives from
ulterior spiritual beings or agencies. If all holy
thoughts and good counsels proceed from a being called God, whence did he derive them?
Why should they not be as ultimate and original
in us, who certainly possess them, as in this
hypothetically constituted author of them?

No doubt on such a view the burden of human responsibility becomes greater, but it is not insupportable. The rule, *Ex nihilo nihil fit*, holds good only in the phenomenal world of matter, and perhaps not absolutely there; and the idea that so much of revelation as there was in Jesus, or as there is in any of us, must needs flow from some ulterior source outside or before us is an illegitimate extension of this rule to the spiritual sphere. Furthermore, we feel that, if Dr. Sanday had not to buttress up the dogma of the two natures in Christ, he would not venture on these excursions into modern philosophy. Now, it is certain that the Fathers of the Church did not mean by their formulas what Professor Sanday tries to make them mean. What, then, is the use of clinging to forms of words which we can no longer take in the sense to express which they were devised? And the same criticism applies to Dr. Gore's explanation of the incarnation as a kenosis or self-emptying by Jesus Christ of his divine nature, as a laying-aside of his cosmic *rôle* and attributes in order to be born a son of woman. Dr. Gore himself allows that no Father or teacher of the Church, from Irenæus down to his friend the late Professor Bright of Oxford, would have tolerated his explanation. Surely, then, it would be better to give up altogether a form of words which he can no longer accept in the sense in which they were framed.

And the same reflection must have crossed the minds of many of the readers of Dr. Sanday's work (already cited) on *Christologies Ancient and Modern* when they reached the passage of it in which he crowns a life of continuous intellectual growth, of ceaseless endeavour to understand others and give them their due, of perpetual and sincere, if cautious, acceptance of Truth as she has unveiled herself to his eyes, with the declaration that he repeats a creed "not as an individual, but as a member of the Church." He does "not feel that he is responsible for" the creeds and "tacitly corrects the defects of expression, because he believes that the Church would correct them if it could." He sums the matter up in the words:

> For the creed as it stands the Church is responsible, and not I. . . . I myself regard the creeds, from this most individual and personal point of view, as great outstanding historical monuments of the Faith of the Church. As such I cannot but look upon them with veneration. . . . But, at the same time, I cannot forget that the critical moments in the composition of the creeds were in the fourth and fifth centuries, and that they have never been revised or corrected since.

As we read these words of Dr. Sanday, we

realise what an advance has taken place in the
last thirty years, and that the day is not far
off when Christian records will be frankly
treated like any other ancient text, and the
gospel narratives taken into general history
to be sifted and criticised according to the same
methods and in the same impartial temper which
we bring to the study of all other documents.
La vérité est en marche.

BIBLIOGRAPHY

[In the following bibliography I confine myself almost entirely to works of the last ten years. It is disconcerting to have to name so few English books; but, as in earlier decades, so in this, the majority of English works bearing on the criticism of the Gospels are merely apologetic, and deserve little notice as works of learning.—F. C. C.]

Abbott, Rev. Edwin A.   All his works.
Bacon, Dr. B. W.   *The Fourth Gospel in Research and Debate.*   New York, 1910.
—— *The Beginnings of Gospel Story.*   Yale, 1909.
Bigg, Canon Ch.   *Wayside Sketches in Ecclesiastical History.*   1906.
Blass, Prof. F.   *Grammar of New Testament Greek.* (Translated by Henry St. John Thackeray.)
Bousset, Prof. Dr. W.   *Hauptprobleme der Gnosis.* 1907.
Burkitt, Prof. F. C.   *Evangelion da-Mepharreshe.* Cambridge, 1904.
Carpenter, Principal Estlin.   *The First Three Gospels.*
Charles, Rev. R. H.   *Eschatology.*   ·London, 1899.
Criticism of the New Testament.   St. Margaret's Lectures.   1902.
Deissmann, Adolf.   *Light from the Ancient East.*   1910.
Dobschütz, E. von.   *The Apostolic Age.*   (Translated by Pogson.)   London, 1910.
Drummond, James.   *Studies in Christian Doctrine.* London. 1909.

Encyclopædia Biblica. Four vols.

Gardner, Prof. Percy. *The Growth of Christianity.* London, 1907.

—— *A Historic View of the New Testament.* 1901.

Gore, Rev. C. H. *Dissertations on the Incarnation.* London, 1895.

Gregory, Dr. C. R. *Canon and Text of the New Testament.* Edinburgh, 1907.

—— *Text kritik des Neuet Testamentes.* Three vols. Leipzig, 1902–1909.

—— *Die Griechischen Handschriften des Neuet Testamentes.* Leipzig, 1908.

—— *Canon and Text of the New Testament.* Edinburgh.

Harnack, A. *Luke the Physician.* (Translated by J. R. Wilkinson.) 1907.

—— *The Sayings of Jesus.* 1908.

Harris, J. Rendell. *Side-lights on New Testament Research.* 1909.

Hastings, James. *Encyclopædia of Religion and Ethics.*

—— *A Dictionary of the Bible.*

Houtin, Albert. *La Question Biblique au XIXe Siècle.* Paris, 1902. And *La Q. B. au XXe Siècle.* Paris, 1906.

The International Critical Commentary. T. & T. Clark, Edinburgh.

Jowett, Benjamin. *Epistles of St. Paul.*

Jülicher, Adolf. *An Introduction to the New Testament.* (Translated by J. P. Ward.) London, 1904.

Knopf, R. *Der Text des Neues Testamentes.* 1906.

Kübel, Johannes. *Geschichte des Katholischen Modernismus.* Tübingen, 1909.

Lake, Prof. Kirsopp. *The Historical Evidence for the Resurrection of Jesus.* 1907.

—— *The Text of the New Testament.* 1900.

Lévy, Albert. *David Frédéric Strauss.* Paris, 1910.

Lietzmann, Hans. *Handbuch zum Neuen Testament.* (In this series are contained Prof. Dr. Paul Wendland's

History of Hellenistic-Roman Culture, and also commentaries on the Gospels and Pauline Epistles.)

Loisy, Alfred. *Les Évangiles Synoptiques.* 1907.

—— *Le Quatrième Évangile.* Paris, 1903.

—— *The Gospel and the Church.* (Translated by C. Home.) 1908.

Macan, R .W. *The Resurrection of Jesus Christ.* Edinburgh, 1877.

McGiffert, A. C. *The Apostles' Creed.* New York, 1902.

—— *History of Christianity in the Apostolic Age.* New York, 1898.

Martineau, James. *The Seat of Authority in Religion.* London, 1890.

Moffatt's *Historical New Testament.*

Montefiore, C. G. *The Synoptic Gospels.* Two vols.

Moulton, James Hope. *A Grammar of New Testament Greek.* Two vols. Edinburgh, 1906.

The New Testament in the Apostolic Fathers. Oxford, 1905.

Pfleiderer, Dr. Otto. *The Early Christian Conception of Christ.* London, 1905.

—— *Primitive Christianity.* (Translated by W. Montgomery.) Two vols.

—— *The Development of Christianity.*

Preuschen, Ed. *Antilegomena.* (Greek texts with German translation.) Second edition. 1905.

The Programme of Modernism. (Translated from the Italian by Rev. A. Leslie Lilley.) 1908.

Ramsay, Sir W. M. *The Church in the Roman Empire, before A.D. 170.*

Reinach, Salomon. *Orpheus.*

Reitzenstein, R. *Die Hellenistischen Mysterienreligionen.* Berlin, 1910.

Renan, E. *Les Apôtres*, 1866; *L'Antechrist*, 1873; *St. Paul.*

Réville, Jean. *Le Quatrième Évangile.* Paris, 1901.

Robinson, Dr. J. A., Dean of Westminster. *The Study of the Gospels.* 1903.

Sabatier, Paul. *Notes d'Histoire religieuse contemporaine, Les Modernistes.* 1909.

Schmiedel, Paul W. *The Johannine Writings.* London, 1908.

Schürer, Prof. Dr. Emil. *History of the Jewish People in the Time of Jesus Christ.*

Schweitzer, Dr. A. *The Quest of the Historical Jesus.* (Translated by W. Montgomery.) 1910.

Smith, Goldwin. *In Quest of Light.* New York, 1906.

Soden, H. von. *History of Early Christian Literature.* (Translated by T. R. Wilkinson.) London, 1906.

Spitta, Prof. Dr. Fr. *Streitfragen der Geschichte Jesus.* 1907.

Sturt, Henry. *The Idea of a Free Church.* London, 1909.

Tyrrell, G. *The Church and the Future.* 1910.

Weizsäcker's *Apostolic Age of the Christian Church.* Two vols.

Wellhausen. *Einleitung in die drei ersten Evangelien.* Berlin, 1905.

Wendt, Prof. Dr. H. H. *Die Lehre Jesu.* 1901.

Wernle, Dr. Paul. *Sources of our Knowledge of the Life of Jesus.* 1907.

—— *The Beginnings of Christianity.* (Translated by G. A. Bienenmann.) 1904.

Westcott and Hort. *Greek Testament.* (With Introduction on the MSS.)

Zahn, Th. *Einleitung in das Neue Testament.* Two vols.

INDEX

A History of the Sciences

¶ Hitherto there have been few, if any, really popular works touching the historical growth of the various great branches of knowledge. The ordinary primer leaves unexploited the deep human interest which belongs to the sciences as contributing to progress and civilization, and calling into play the faculties of many of the finest minds. Something more attractive is wanted.

¶ The above need in literature has now been met. Each volume in *The History of Sciences* is written by an expert in the given subject, and by one who has studied the history as well as the conclusions of his own branch of science. The monographs deal briefly with the myths or fallacies which preceded the development of the given science, or include biographical data of the great discoverers. Consideration is given to the social and political conditions and to the attitudes of rulers

G. P. Putnam's Sons

New York   London

A History of the Sciences

and statesmen in furthering or in hindering the progress of the given science. The volumes record the important practical application of the given science to the arts and life of civilized mankind, and also contain a carefully-edited bibliography of the subject. Each volume contains from twelve to sixteen carefully-prepared illustrations, including portraits of celebrated discoverers, many from originals not hitherto reproduced, and explanatory views and diagrams. The series as planned should cover in outline the whole sphere of human knowledge.

¶ Science is to be viewed as a product of human endeavor and mental discipline, rather than taken in its purely objective reference to facts. The essential purpose has been to present as far as practicable the historical origins of important discoveries, also to indicate the practical utility of the sciences to human life.

G. P. Putnam's Sons

New York   London

A History of the Sciences

Each volume is adequately illustrated, attractively printed, and substantially bound.

16mo. Each, net, 75 cents. By mail, 85 cents. 12 illustrations

History of Astronomy

By George Forbes, M.A., F.R.S., M.Inst. C.E.

Formerly Professor of Natural Philosophy, Anderson's College, Glasgow

I thank you for the copy of Forbes's *History of Astonomy* received. I have run it over, and think it very good indeed. The plan seems excellent, and I would say the same of your general plan of a series of brief histories of the various branches of science. The time appears to be ripe for such a series, and if all the contributions are as good as Prof. Forbes's, the book will deserve a wide circulation, and will prove very useful to a large class of readers.—*Extract from a letter received from Garrett P. Serviss, B.S.*

History of Chemistry

By Sir Edward Thorpe, C.B., LL.D., F.R.S.

Author of "Essays in Historical Chemistry," "Humphry Davy: Poet and Philosopher," "Joseph Priestley," etc.

12 illustrations. Two vols. Vol. I—circa 2000 B.C. to 1850 A.D. Vol. II—1850 A.D. to date

The author traces the evolution of intellectual thought in the progress of chemical investigation, recognizing the various points of view of the different ages, giving due credit even to the ancients. It has been necessary to curtail many parts of the History, to lay before the reader in unlimited space enough about each age to illustrate its tone and spirit, the ideals of the workers, the gradual addition of new points of view and of new means of investigation.

The History of Old Testament Criticism

By Archibald Duff

Professor of Hebrew and Old Testament Theology in the United College, Bradford

The author sets forth the critical views of the Hebrews concerning their own literature, the early Christian treatment of the Old Testament, criticism by the Jewish rabbis, and criticism from Spinoza to Astruc, and from Astruc until the present.

The History of Anthropology.

By A. C. HADDON, M.A., Sc.D., F.R.S., Lecturer in Ethnology, Cambridge and London.

In Preparation

The History of Geography.

By Dr. JOHN SCOTT KELTIE, F.R.G.S., F.S.A., Hon. Mem. Geographical Societies of Paris, Berlin, Rome, Brussels, Amsterdam, Geneva, etc.

The History of Geology.

By HORACE B. WOODWARD, F.R.S., F.G.S., Assistant Director of Geological Survey of England and Wales.

The History of New Testament Criticism.

By F. C. CONYBEARE, M.A., late Fellow and Praelector of Univ. Coll., Oxford; Fellow of the British Academy; Doctor of Theology, *honoris causa*, of Giessen; Officer d'Academie.

Further volumes are in plan on the following subjects:

Mathematics and Mechanics—Molecular Physics, Heat, Light, and Electricity—Human Physiology, Embryology, and Heredity—Acoustics, Harmonics, and the Physiology of Hearing, together with Optics, Chromatics, and Physiology of Seeing—Psychology, Analytic, Comparative, and Experimental—Sociology and Economics—Ethics—Comparative Philology— Criticism, Historical Research, and Legends—Comparative Mythology and the Science of Religions— The Criticism of Ecclesiastical Institutions—Culture, Moral and Intellectual, as Reflected in Imaginative Literature and in the Fine Arts—Logic—Philosophy —Education.

New York G. P. Putnam's Sons London

SD - #0038 - 131224 - C0 - 229/152/12 - PB - 9781330847527 - Gloss Lamination